STAYING WOMAN
Living Life By Design

By Tamara Marcella

Introduction

L et me start by saying that everything about you, woman, is beautiful! Your faults, failures and weaknesses—are all beautiful. Because in them are the makings of a woman who is being equipped to be the perfect expression of "you." Every part He uses, every measure He infuses. From start to finish, He ordered your steps from conception to this very moment as you read this book. Your Father, who designed you, has spoken over your life, blessing it, saying,."It is good."

We fight every day the distractions and clever ways the enemy has come to dismantle and mar the image that God has already said is good. We believe the lying words of the enemy over the truth of the sovereign creator. Speaking as a designer, for example, I'm quite sure that Michael Kors is not concerned about what others say about his designs ! So it is with God. Your Father in heaven has designed you for a purpose and a specific use. He chose in eternity's past to use you and to do something unique for you. God does not search the earth to find a man, or a woman . To have them manifest His will on earth; He raises them up, and He has already determined your success.

Now is the time for you to settle the issues that clutter your heart. That thing that happened that you're still holding on to, the way you were born, the abandonment, whatever it is, settle it. God can use it and I know it's not popular, but God grafts it into your destiny. The lies of deception cause you to carry guilt, shame and suffering due to an emotional tie to your struggle. Today you can be released from the need to make sense of it. You can't understand the parental need for us to endure hurt and discomfort. It's beyond your level of human comprehension. It's God's needlework, weaving in the good, the bad and the ugly, creating a tapestry of elegance that perfectly expresses God's glory. The energy that rises from the heart, rising out of tragedy, is tremendous. It's called passion, fire, or anointing.

God takes a tragic situation and writes a story of victory and love. He takes a crazy day of mommy struggles and leaves you with a lesson. He allows workplace battles to build in you a CEO. At the center of it all is a woman — you. You were chosen for this moment and developed in time. God takes a fragile heart and unites it with the perfect measure of strength, and creates hope.

Allow hope to drive you into purpose. Right now would be a good time to take a moment to thank God for everything you've walked through, lived through, and are going through, yet survived. None of it will be wasted. Every tear you cried will be acknowledged, and every hurt you endured will be acknowledged. Not one mistake you've made will be wasted, nor past failures. It's your story of glory!

1

Women in the Making

"She took of the fruit and ate." Eve's "epic fail," is found in the pages of stories, coffee discussions, and of course sermons preached throughout time and around the world. Locked within her story of betrayal, lust and timeless consequence lies a beautiful depiction of God's deep desire for fellowship, grace and mercy. A glorious picture of unity and oneness in a covenant relationship between a husband and wife. At the same time, it portrays the sad reality of how quickly and devastating can be the repercussions of an interruption to that oneness. Her purpose, her place and her significance were in God's plan, both in the earth and in the covenant institution of marriage. His intent was for duel dominion in childrearing and in creation, the marketplace and in ministry. This is a message too often omitted in the epilogue.

Although created a weaker vessel, Eve was in every way capable of the task for which she had been created. She was created a helper suitable in every way for Adam. Let me share with you a few synonyms in our English language depicting the word "suitable." There's fitting, sufficient, relevant and proper. You will also find handy or useful. The English language makes clear on its own the fact that Eve was designed to walk side by side with Adam in tandem ministry. She was designed to fulfill and complete her purpose and assist Adam in his. She certainly would not have been a help to Adam if she was created any less. Every good leader knows that for a job to be done properly, it is required that you put in place the right people who are equipped for assisting. People whose ability and mental capacity both complement the team.

Genesis 1:26

And God said, let us make man in our image,
after our likeness: and let them have dominion

over the fish of the sea, and over the fowl of the air, and over all the earth, and over every creeping thing that creepeth upon the earth.

Wow, that is certainly a mouthful, and a powerfully packed statement. First of all, let's note that mankind had not been created yet. This was a sneak peek into a conversation between the Godhead. We see the Trinity in conversation. Notice what God said: "in our image, after our likeness" create "them." Eve, too? Oh yes! Eve too was created in the image of God and in the likeness of Him, and planned before the creation of humanity. Within the Trinity there is found all the nature and characteristics in both man and woman.

Am I saying that any one of the Trinity is female? Absolutely not! Yet our feminine qualities came from the very nature of God. Our ability to comfort, deeply grieve, and to nurture echo qualities describing the Holy Spirit. In fact, the exact same word originally used to define "helper" was also used to describe the promised Holy Spirit, sent to God's covenant people. This was said of the Holy Spirit: *"So let me say this again, this truth: it*

11

is better for you that I leave. If I don't leave, the friend won't come. But if I go, I'll send him to you." John 16:7 message This is the value that Jesus placed on the need for mankind, God's covenant people, to have the Holy Spirit to dwell in us and do life with us. That was the plan of God. Mankind working together as a dynamic duo.

I hope by now you have begun to see that Eve represented a need in the Earth and in humanity that only she could fulfill. There really is no competition between the two genders when one understands the original purpose for the "two." Eve was part of the need. Even her weakness, if you will, was part of the need. Could it be that I would imply that Eve's fall was part of the design? I recognize that this will be a controversial point, but God's grace and mercy could have never been realized in the Earth if Eve had never fallen. And since Jesus is The Lamb slain "before" the foundation of the earth, could it be that what was formerly taught as Eve's epic fail may have been "The Epic Plan"?

Consider the fact that in **Jeremiah 1:5,** God said, *"Before I formed you in the womb I knew you, And before you were* *born I consecrated you; I have appointed you a prophet to the nations."* <u>Before I formed you.</u> That means that before you were a person, God had a need for you to come. In other words, your purpose preceded your person. Everything in your life, including your conception, was purposed. God never does anything without purpose. Including creation. He created humanity to fellowship with the Father, to worship Him and for His absolute glory.

You, as a part of humanity, the feminine part, serve a God-given purpose. You were not an afterthought, nor a fulfillment of Adam's sexual needs. You were created and purposed for God's glory. Your description and image of what femininity is may have been derived from a lifetime of images that shaped your view of what that is, but God is the **designer** of women. He is the only one with the right to call that design by name, and He did... It's called **woman**.

No one, no human should be announcing your description, naming or defining you, because it has already been done. Losing that description is a prescription for all sorts of failure. It makes you susceptible to self-degradation and verbal mutilation, both from others you are involved with and your own verbal annihilation, which is most convincing.

Your design and destiny come from the Designer, the one who predetermined your worth. He predetermined your value and set into place your limitless potential. He organized a set of footprints that only you could walk through. He put into motion a destiny human minds cannot comprehend. A destiny unscripted by human hands. It's amazing, it's wonderful, it's beautiful, it's you.

"Eye has not seen, nor ear heard, Nor have entered into the heart of man the things which God has prepared for those who love Him. 1 Corinthians 2:9

Your purpose exists. It existed before you. Even if you feel like you missed it, because it tarries you're just waiting for the great unveiling, the manifestation.

God is waiting for you to "become" the person capable of holding the purpose. To be the woman God called you to "be" is paramount to you walking in your purpose.

Remember the children of Israel. They weren't prevented from reaching the Promised Land due to the difficulties in the journey. God was faithful to carry them where they needed to go. He brought them through the wilderness, confident they could make the journey. In fact, He planned to sustain them through the wilderness experience, and use the time to develop them.

2"You shall remember all the way which the LORD your God has led you in the wilderness these forty years, that He might humble you, testing you, to know what was in your heart, whether you would keep His commandments or not. 3 He humbled you and let you be hungry, and fed you with manna which you did not know, nor did your fathers know, that He might make you understand that man does not live by bread alone, but man lives by everything

15

that proceeds out of the mouth of the LORD."

Deuteronomy 8;2

The Father's intent was to show them a relationship with Him? That was not the same old relationship their forefathers had. He desired to bring them into an experience of their own. God wants you to meet Him in your journey, learning of all He has for you along the way. Not living the relationship you heard about someone having. Not even the same relationship your pastor, husband or father had. This is a relationship unique to the life God has planned for you. He uses the hungry moments of life to drive you into His presence, so that He might sustain you with life-giving bread. These include issues that would create opportunities that would expose what is in your heart, obstacles that would solidify in your mind ... YOU NEED HIM! EVERY DAY! And He is there by your side.

What interrupted their call was their inability to conquer self. They failed to become the people who were able to possess the land. Remember the migration through the wilderness? At every turn, they groaned and mourned leaving Egypt, questioning God's intent for them. God brought them out of slavery and saved them from a tyrannical king. They couldn't see the value of the process.

While the journey was difficult, God made preparation for them. He supplied manna in the wilderness. A miracle was sent every day to teach them trust and absolute dependency on Him. He showed them that in the midst of their struggle, He was not just the God of Moses, but He was their God, too. The unrelenting perils caused contempt rather than trust. Unable to be challenged and developed, the Promised Land remained afar off. They never received their promise! Difficult as it is to understand, they thwarted their destiny by refusing to grow in the process. Nothing in the journey prevented the promise!

Joshua and Caleb, the Bible says, were of a "different spirit." A spirit determined not to give up in the journey God designed. They learned to trust God and flowed in the fellowship of intimacy God longed for, on the road to promise. When faced with obstacles, they chose to trust God.

God wants you to become a woman capable of possessing His promise for you. He desires for you to enter into true fellowship with Him. The journey you are on is growing and training you for exploits. Learn to lean on Him in the process.

Destiny is a journey ... a destination, not an event.

2

He Chooses You

I'm too old, too broke, and have too many issues and failures in my life. I've been through too much. I wasn't raised in the church. I have a battery of failed relationships. I'm just not that kind of woman. Sound like some of your thoughts? Well, God isn't afraid of your failures or your excuses. **You are.**

The truth is, you may believe your feelings of indecency and low self-worth are unique to you. Or your struggle with believing that at this point in your life God would take your past and life course to do anything beyond the ordinary may be difficult. Daring to dream outside of this extremely mundane lifestyle, intermittent chaos, and the dishes you wash would stretch faith. You are in good company. What if I told you some of the things you call failure are merely set-ups for God to show off in your life? To bring you to a place where you hunger and thirst for Him? To drive you to a place where you find yourself hiding out in the shadows of His wings? Perhaps you're reading this right now, saying, "That sound great, Tamara, but you don't know what I did or where I've been. You don't know the obstacles I face. You don't know the upbringing I had. The husband I have or don't have. I'm alone and I'm too ugly or too fat. Etc."

It's true, I don't! But I know that whatever you wrote in the pages of your life leading up to this moment, like pop singer Natasha Bedingfeild said, "The rest is still unwritten"!! I can tell you that I know many stories that must come close to your story.

Try this story: There, stuck in the middle of her seemingly unchanged day, was a woman headed to the well. It was her custom to go get water for the day around the same time each day. On her way, she arrived at the well to meet up with a man who seemed interested in what she was doing. He asked her, "Can you draw some water for me?" A bit bewildered about why this Jew would talk to a SAMARITAN, in those days the hatred between the jews and the Samaritans ran deep. With Israel and Samaria divided, cultural, religious and ethnic differences continued to separate them as a people . Though living along side each other a great distain remained prevalent in their community. They both desired to keep separate to prevent any further mixing of the people and culture. She reluctantly drew some water from the well and gave it to the gentleman. What seemed at first a normal chore, the daily grind, turned out to be a destiny moment. She was aware of the oddness of the moment, but unaware of where it would lead.

As quickly as it began, she was sharing her deepest, darkest secrets with this stranger. He asked her, "Go and get your husband ." This question caused a bit of anxiety, because now she would have to admit the truth, that she had no husband. While searching for love, she had compromised and engaged in a cycle of revolving male companionship in her life, leading to shame and degradation. While still reserved about the questions from the stranger, his reply brought some ambiguity, but still she felt the grace within his words. She wasn't sure why he asked, but she believed she could trust him.

"He told me all that I had done and who I was." John 4;29
Yet in spite of what he knew about her, he noticed her. His love
was healing her right there at the well. All the shame associated with the fear of exposure melted away as he spoke to her
concerning her secrets. He instantly broke her free from the
power of the past.

God doesn't need to erase your past to use you. But he does
need to break the chains that hold you to the past. He wants you
healed from the pain of it.

To return to the story: The thoughts that would keep her
in a cycle of perpetually allowing herself to be used by men,
lowering her standard of self-worth, needed to change, so she
would no longer see herself as an object to be used. The fact
that this man would know her "stuff" and still see value in her
was overwhelming.

Everyone has failures associated with their past. It's never
God's plan for His daughters to remain there, paralyzed in the
pain and tied to the shame. When Jesus seeks to encounter
every one of us at the well, that might be the time to heal you

and let you know **He chooses you**! In spite of what you did, where you've been, He chooses you.

At the start of the Samaritan woman's journey to the well, she was broken, but she left completely freed of an identity that had been influenced by her life decisions. She was now completely ready and able to carry out her new adventure of sharing her testimony of how she met the Savior at the well. The Savior who knew her inside and out waited for her and chose her.

What hope is there in God having to remove or erase your past to for you to be acceptable to Him? The beauty of our Savior is the absolute glory of the gospel, which is that God knows you inside and out. He knows your failures and has seen your life, and still He waits and calls you. You can be healed of your past and do great things for God, just like the woman at the well.

I pray that you meet Jesus at the well. Maybe you haven't been on a path of bad choices, but have gotten so locked into routine, and mundane living with no joy that you missed Jesus trying to intersect your path and meet with you. For you, too,

He waits. He desires to turn your days into fruitful progress, where you see His hand in your life.

There's another woman I want to tell you about, a woman with a past that some would believe would have been rendered her useless to the kingdom, if it weren't for the redeeming God we serve.

Entrenched in the realities of an unconventional career, a woman named Rahab finds herself in a destiny moment herself. Her lifestyle was no secret to the townspeople. Known as the innkeeper, Rahab was certainly an innkeeper with certain benefits for those who could afford to pay. In those days, she was called a harlot. Prostitute, today. Contrary to what her occupation would suggest, no one could deny that Rahab had had a revelation of the true Savior. Would our Savior give a revelation of Himself to a harlot? While harboring and keeping safe the men of God, Rahab uttered this statement, a confession of faith: "For the Lord your God is the God in heaven and on earth" Joshua 2;11 This woman, though a harlot, still had an understanding who the one true God was.

She lied to ensure the spies' safe departure from town. But before they left, she met them on the roof to ask for safety for her family, a return on the favor she had provided. A small request, a life for a life. She was given the promise that if she hung a red cord outside the window, all who were in her house would be saved. Rahab could not have known the devastation that she and her family could have faced. Yet she willingly reached out to help the spies on their way. Risking her life, she proved to be a hero!

So held in favor, she is noted as a woman of faith, celebrated and loved by Salmon, who took her as his wife. This former harlot ended up in the Christ's family tree, and gave birth to a son who would have no doubt been chosen for America's most desired and eligible bachelor; Boaz. An honorable mention would be given her in the book of Hebrews among the greats of faith.

Clearly, a past doesn't have to define your future. God is a God who redeems and knows all. Somehow, some way, the God of the universe sovereignly chooses to know us and use us flawed human beings. Rahab was a woman with a sordid background, but was also a courageous one, with fearless acts of heroism. God used this woman to deliver His men.

Can God do great things through women? You bet!

Even broken women! Absolutely!

In case you were tempted to think they were flukes, despite thinking that because you chose a man who is not a believer, or maybe you had a child out of wedlock, despite what you may have been told or what conclusion you have arrived at, you can still be a great parent and raise godly kids. You can do it even as a single parent. All by yourself if you have to.

We read in the scripture about Timothy, a young man of faith who either had no dad around or an unbelieving dad who wasn't very relevant in his life. Without a father as a role model, amazingly, he still became a great man. Paul came to call him into ministry at a young age, admonishing and advising him on all the issues he would need to be briefed on. *"Don't let others look down on you because of your youth."* 1 Timothy 4;12 Then Paul threw in credit to his mother and grandmother for the faith that was passed down to him. These were two women who didn't allow their circumstance to dictate the future of their lives or their son and grandson. This was a young man full of faith and character because of two women. Two women who didn't allow the obstacle or the craziness that threatened their success to stop them. They as women raised a boy. Not with gender issues, not with insecurities, just respect.

"But you must continue in the things which you have learned and been assured of, knowing from whom you have learned them, and that from childhood you have known the Holy Scriptures, which are able to make you wise for salvation through faith which is in Christ Jesus." **2 Timothy 3:14-15**

"I call to remembrance the genuine faith that is in you, which dwelt first in your grandmother Lois and your mother Eunice, and I am persuaded is in you also." (2 Timothy 1:5) Women of faith, against the odds raised a young man to be great. Never let your temporary situation, become the barometer for the rest of your life.

The list of great women God used to achieve exploits goes on. Your name is in there too. Modern times haven't changed that fact. God is still in the business of raising up women to do great things for Him. He chooses women still, through faith and failure, through a tough hand of cards and undesired circumstances. Maybe you will raise children for God, right there in your own home. Not rich, not famous, but an awesome mom. That is so needed. It's the forgotten career. Homemakers!!!

I know some moms who don't dream of being anything but an exceptional mom, and they are doing it with excellence. I have a dear girlfriend who inspires me daily to be a better mom on the days I feel like I've failed, maybe said the wrong thing, done the wrong thing. She dusts me off and sends me back into the game. She's bringing up children for God and doing exactly what God has instructed us to do: raise children in the fear and admonition of God.

Maybe you were called to be an apostle or in the ministry, like Phoebe, a world-changer like Esther, or ugly like Leah, yet after years of searching for love in all the wrong places you find yourself nestled into an intimate reality of who your Savior is. Finding a heart that worships Him. You could be a shining example of loyalty and selflessness, like Ruth, dedicated to sticking by Naomi, with no regard for her personal reward. Found serving in a field, she was later taken to be Boaz's wife in one of the coolest Cinderella stories of the Bible. From the field to the mansion.

What if you start out barren like Hanna? What if you become proof of the fact that God is still doing the miraculous? Could you be the one who shows those around you how to find yourself on the altar? Even though you hurt. Even though you feel like everything you touch in life has become bitter, because all you want is a child you fear will never come? Could you perform courageous kinds of worship, worshiping God when you don't have what you want? Then when He honors you and gives you the miracle, you turn around and give it back to Him. That is priceless. Is that you? Does the potential for deep gratitude, in spite of your past, drive you to the feet of Jesus like Mary Magdalene? Do you carry Christ inside you, like His mother?

Whatever it is, whatever your calling, no amount of past failures or mistakes could ever change that! Flawed, ugly or broken, find the hope of glory inside you. Christ! Because He lives, He reigns, and He pre-determined to give you the seat of honor with Him, you too can reign. You can rule this life with promise and purity, no matter what your past.

I would be remiss if I ended this chapter without the words of the Samaritan woman at the well: "He knows me inside and out."

3

The Limp

I n the earlier chapters, I mentioned how we already have a definition, a perfect design that life experiences fight to alter. Every now and then, we women find ourselves adapting and relating to life through those areas God healed us of with residual effects. I refer to it as the limp. The pains and hurts we've gone through cause us to walk a little crocked. The *Webster's Dictionary* gives this definition for the word limp: *a. To walk lamely; especially: to walk favoring one leg b. to go unsteadily: falter 2. to proceed slowly or with difficulty ...*

You can limp from the way your mother treated you, or your father not being there. Maybe it was a husband who betrayed you, or a friend. I know I've limped from hurtful things said to me. I've limped from financial struggles I've encountered. You proceed through life slower now because this hurt and pain caused a limp in your life. You may have been living with this limp so long that you don't even notice that you walk with a limp. But I'm quite sure that those around you see the limp. Everything you do and say is now filtered through that limp. The way you parent. The way you relate to your spouse. The way you work. Even the way you relate to God.

I remember one season of my life. I realized that my limp was mistrust. I had experienced some betrayal in my life by some people I dearly loved. In my younger years, if I was hurt, I could walk away. So I walked away. The problem was that as I grew older, relationships were more valuable to me. God was requiring more of me. I had to stay and deal with pain and hurt. I had to learn to forgive in a way I hadn't before. During the process of the healing, I had developed a limp. I had begun to favor those areas of my heart affected by betrayal. Subsequently, I treated everyone like they were a suspect. I took no one at their word, including God!

One day I was in my prayer time, talking to our Father, struggling with some things He said He would do for me. I couldn't even receive answered prayer because I was so unsteady in my walk. My limp determined how I related to words that were spoken to me. I constantly needed God to reiterate and coddle me. One day He responded with a stern, "I AM NOT A MAN THAT I SHOULD LIE." Wow!!!! I realized that I was even making God pay for the limp that I had taken on. Well, healing began at that very moment. I was so overcome with sadness about what I had become.

He ministered to me everything He had said to me before, only now I could actually receive it. He helped me to understand that "when you know better, you do better." I was holding people accountable for the hurt they caused in *my* life out of a lack of understanding, but I had become a person who was dishing out hurt and mistrust also. I made everyone pay for the misdeeds of a few. The limp was actually destroying my relationships and certainly rendering me unusable for God.

You may be recognizing a limp in your own life right now. For me, the road between recognition and healing of that limp was a long one. Honestly, I wasn't ready. It felt good to have a reason to be angry. It made sense that I would be a little wounded from hurt. God showed me how possible it was to start getting over the pain right away.

My mouth was the link between my being stuck and the glue coming off. God showed me that the confessions of my mouth needed to change. I had been saying, "I can't get over it. I just can't see how I could ever move beyond this place." Subsequently, healing wasn't close. If I ever wanted to walk straight again, I had to begin confessing healing. I started saying things like, "I'm almost over it," and "I'm further along today than I was yesterday." I started creating passwords into my computer like, "I am healed," so every time I turned on my computer I had to declare, "I am healed," and you know what? Before I knew it, I was healed.

I was able to love and live. I was able to trust even those who had desperately hurt and betrayed me. In a short period of time, no more limp. I walked steady. I loved steady. I could trust the words God spoke to me. I could believe in new beginnings. You have to make a decision to be healed. Then the journey of healing starts. That may seem impossible for it to really be that simple. You make the decision to walk normal again, and the healing will follow.

The crippled man lay at the pool of Bethesda, waiting for someone to come along and drop him into the pool when the waters were stirring. Jesus came along and asked him, "Do you want to be made well?" Why would He have to ask someone who was crippled, lying on a cot at the very place, the very edge of healing, "Do you want to be made well?" Scripture makes it clear that the man lay there for thirty-eight years. Nothing had changed in thirty-eight years!

Wow, how many years have you had the same issue functioning, holding you back? Angry about something that happened ten years ago? Maybe you're still holding onto something your parents did or didn't do forty years ago? Whatever it is that is crippling you, one question can break open the healing waters. "Do you want to be made well?"

This man had to stop making someone else responsible for his healing, the holder of his change, the destiny accountant. His healing was only in **his** hands. It was his job to decide if he wanted to be well. It was his job to make a life change. How many marriages are damaged, even ended because people live in relationships with limps?

Walking with a limp was not open to discussion for the woman with the issue of blood. She went to doctors, she did everything in her power to get rid of her infirmity. She decided, "If I just touch the great healer, I will be made well." She decided that she was going put her faith into action and get her healing. So she fought her way through a crowd. She was determined! She was motivated! She was inspired to go after what she needed to live life without her limp.

So she finally got to Jesus and she touched just the hem of His garment. Instantly she was healed. In fact, Jesus stopped His movement through the crowd to say, "Who touched me?" The disciples were amazed by this question, because after all, He was in a crowd of people. Jesus said, "Healing power went forth from me." When He found her, He said to her, "Woman, your faith has made you whole."

You must make up your mind about whether or not you want to be made well. If you are tired of living life with a limp, then **today** you make the decision to be made well.

When I say that you can be great for God, sometimes there is a misconception that that means you must be rich or famous, or travel the nations, or do some extraordinary thing. No, being great for God is simply living your live without any limps, loving your God with a life of worship. Everything you do is worship. So you honor God at your job, in your relationships, and in your church.

Raise your kids without limps. How many people are parenting through a limp of the past? God wants you to be able to live peaceable. To do that, today starts the day that you identify your limps, and without excuses, you take them to God and ask Him to heal you. Like the woman with the issue of blood, just be determined about your healing. Don't allow yourself another day to put it off and rationalize the whys. No, get to Jesus and get your healing. You will never be more at peace in this life as you will be when you get serious about your healing.

Jesus gave the man at the pool of Bethesda a few simple commands. He said, "Get up." You can't lay there anymore. You can't ask God for healing and turn around and lie back down, or go back to your old ways of mistrust. Every area where you functioned with a limp before, you must now learn to walk steady. Get up.

It's been said that you don't have to be great to start, but you do have to start to be great. Well, I say you don't have to feel healed to start, but you do have to start if you ever want to feel healed. So just get up, put one foot in front of the other, and start walking out life without that limp. Oh, you're going to feel the stress from that fracture. I shattered my ankle once, and after I came out of the cast and started walking, it was months into the journey that my ankle, though healed, struggled to stretch. It screamed at me when I did things I used to do with ease before. It had to essentially learn to walk all over again. Even though I felt pain at times. I knew that I had to work through the pain. I knew I had to continue to stretch my muscles to the point of pain if I wanted to walk and run normally again.

You're going to feel the same thing as you learn to walk without that emotional limp in your life. You're going to experience moments of stress in those muscles. They are going to scream at you in pain and they are going to fight you to release the pressure. But if you don't make a determined effort to get up, you will lie there on that cot for thirty more years — but you should know that you'll lie there with the full knowledge of your choice. You'll be choosing to walk the rest of your life with a limp.

The next command Jesus gave the man at Bethesda was, "Take up your pallet." He was really saying, "Now clean up your mess." Imagine lying on a cot for thirty-eight years. He probably desperately needed a shower. He probably had all kinds of mess associated with lying in one place. Well, Jesus was saying, "Clean up your mess."

When I realized that my limp was mistrust, I had to give some apologies. My poor husband lived many years with me treating him like he was a liar, due to my limp. My friends, my family, I couldn't take anyone's word for anything. I was suspicious and realized that wasn't really loving. So my cleaning up myself meant telling people I was sorry. I wasn't going to treat them all like liars anymore.

I also had to start talking again to some folks who I said I would never have a relationship with because they hurt me. Well, some people are toxic, and getting away from them is what you need to do. But for me, in that case I was claiming I had forgiven them, but acted as though they didn't exist. That's not forgiving. In my case, I knew God wanted me to show the love of God to this person, even though they hurt me. In spite of the fact they betrayed me, I had learned to love again. God increased in me a capacity to love that was miraculous. I could love and understand their pain. No longer only seeing my side, I saw through the eyes of love their brokenness, their limp, which ultimately was the reason they betrayed me in the first place.

Hurting people hurt people! As I walked out the task of cleaning up my mess, God began to restore things in my life that I don't believe ever could have been restored, had I not been determined to be made well. So pick up your cot!! Start cleaning up your mess. Forgive, if you must. Move on where you need to move on. Start trusting if you need to trust. Call that friend and talk through your issue. Whatever you need to do to start cleaning up your mess, do it.

Then Jesus' last command was ....WALK!!! Walk into your new healing. Walk into your future. Be the woman God designed you to be, with no limps.

4

Henhouse Roles

B attles between the sexes are creeping into homes. The world sends out ugly messages and the church preaches silliness that continues to impede progression. Single ladies try to maintain their identities and hold on to who they want to be — as if marriage was ever intended to deplete rather than enhance. Something is causing them to think that they can't be strong, determined and called, yet married. Men who refuse to take their place promote the issues that erode. This creates an avidity among women to function in dual roles, or creates such a hostile environment where dominance plays the leading role.

The issues that plague harmony between genders can only continue to grow, until enough has been taught to dispel the lies we are being told. Unfortunately, this also lends itself to women shrinking back from their potential in society, churches, homes and the marketplace. The world pays the price. If God placed something deep down inside you, it is your purpose and it's incumbent upon you to pick a man who will be able to walk alongside that call. I read a quote on Facebook one day that said, "You date at the level of your self-esteem." Oh, how true this is. It's a problem so complex with generational impact.

When two people clearly understand their purpose and potential in life, completed by a genuine love for one another, they do everything they can do to help the other become everything they desire to be and feel called to do. If you have a husband or boyfriend who doesn't push you into progress and challenge you to grow, he is not being the man God intended him to be. You would be remiss to lay down your dreams. Keep dreaming and moving confidently in the direction of your dreams, and let him catch up. We will not enter heaven answering to God for our lives two by two. It's going to be you and God. You will have to give an account for the deeds done in your body. You alone are going to have to explain to God why

43

you choose not to complete the tasks He asked you to complete. Let no one be in control of your destiny.

However, my husband is my husband because we have entered into covenant to walk out our destinies together. I cheerlead for him and he does the same for me. Love always wants what's best for the other. God's plan for promotion is achieved by sacrifice. Jesus gave the greatest example. He came to Earth and gave His life. He knew no sin, yet became sin for all those given to Him by the Father. He felt separation from the Father for the first ever because of it, yet chose it so that you and I would be lifted up. He died so we might live.

That's the example of how love treats another in application. No, we are not perfect like Jesus, but we should be aiming to get close. Our husbands should hold this as their standard of how to view whose dream, whose call comes first. The wife should have the same view. For if they both approach a union with that perspective, both will be able to rise and take hold of all God has prepared.

"I can be it all, do it all, and I don't need a man." This is the lie I heard. I bought it. I almost believed it. Haven't you

heard? So many confuse being a strong women with being "that woman" who thinks she doesn't need a man, but always has one. This is another misconception. Being strong women doesn't means that we are in competition with men. We grow up looking for love, watching stories of romance, and seeking the men of ours dreams. Then we are sold this lie that men are our rivals and we had better dominate them before they dominate us. Movies echoed the tone in this matter by portraying the heroines in movies as women beating up men.

Churches preach submission as if it's synonymous with slavery, and the whole idea becomes illuminated and distorted. We are hosting discussions as to whether or not women are called. Can they preach, can they speak? God forbid they have something to say in disagreement with their spouses. Then they are Jezebels and pagans. Hence the war between the sexes continues.

Strength is not a negative, it's a plus. It's part of the ingredient that makes us women. We were created one part strong, the other part sweet. Strength rightly understood never leads us to compete.

There's a story about a woman named Deborah who was not only strong, she served alongside men. Strength wasn't her only asset. Wisdom also hovered close. She was a leader and prophetess who spoke wisdom into the lives of women and men at a time when it was even less common for men to seek counsel from a woman. Deborah rose to a place of social prominence because she was exceptional.

There was a battle to fight that clearly appeared to be destined to fail. She and her troops were outnumbered and ill-equipped. Uninhibited by the outlandish situation, she proceeded forward and found a well trained General and shared with him how he could win the war. Although this seemed a mission starkly close to David's Goliath, she rose to the occasion with a plan that won the battle. No one was like Deborah in all the land, incredible strength of character, strong in her being. Yet she was a woman. If strength was not a "personality" of a woman, Deborah didn't know about it.

Her wisdom gave her the grace to also be humble. Barak the general was determined to let Deborah lead the troops. He had developed such a confidence in her that he didn't want to go without her. She told him, "Then they will say a woman won the battle." She encouraged him to go and lead the troops, but she agreed to go alongside him. Somehow I don't think Barak was intimidated by Deborah's strength of character. It was to his benefit to praise it, to allow its full spans to develop and grow. Real men would never fear or seek to demand the strength in you to diminish. Quite the contrary. Deborah was great and served alongside a man who knew who he was. The result was that Deborah arose and a war was won.

Jael likewise was an example of a woman of strength, yet very much a woman. In fact, it was her femininity that assisted her in her challenge. She was a princess warrior if there ever was one. She met up with Sisera, the enemy general, one who would be equated with Osama Bin Ladan today. She brought him into her tent, where she wined him and dined him. She treated him so well that he fell asleep from exhaustion. Jael knew what needed to be done, and the importance of the moment. With no further hesitation, she drew from every bit of courage she had left. Thinking on her feet, she grabbed a tent peg and drove it through Sisera's head, killing her guest and the enemy of the land instantly.

She was hailed a national heroine. There was no room in her life to be less than who she was. She went on to pursue the Israelite forces, led by the fierce Deborah and Barak. Women, you can and should be strong. There are lots of women who are called to extreme areas of great potential, who also have men in their lives. Love creates a beautiful atmosphere of growth and pride for that strength and calling. Never be afraid to shine. Being who you are should never take away from who any son of the king can also be.

While competition is not the attitude of the strong, issues surrounding it can cause trouble in relationships.

This reminds me of a little hen in my henhouse. She took on the role of being a rooster, though very much a hen. No matter how well she thought she was doing the job, she was not a rooster and everyone else in the henhouse was confused about the role she stole. As devastating as it was to the overall health of the flock, the saddest part was that while that hen was so busy trying to *be* the rooster and compete for the role of rooster, she stopped performing her *hen* role. The job she had been placed there to do was going neglected. I'm not sure what provoked this behavior or why she found herself in this role crisis, but her role crisis isn't unique to her.

There is an entire social structure revolving around this scenario. For one reason or another, women are playing the role of fathers, and are unable to adequately be the mothers they were intended to be. They struggle with their feminine identity when they are forced to occupy two roles in in the home. Whether you are husbandless or the husband there is non-functioning, the complexities of this type of role mixture are unchaining.

Fear can motivate the hen/rooster crisis. However, usually there are more than one complicated reason we vie for the rooster's role. We find ourselves in a quandary about the competence of the men we've chosen. How do you find solace in being a hen in the flock when the rooster in your coop is not very proficient? The temptation comes to seize the role while tearing up the muck in the hen house.

Journey through this scenario with me. What does a rooster do when his role is taken over by another? In a normal henhouse, the fewer roosters there are, the better. Typically there is one rooster to every five hens, depending on the breed. The job of the rooster is to protect the flock, keep order, and obviously reproduce. Years ago, I had a couple of roosters in my henhouse. One of them was a beautiful white silkie who was a sight to see. If looks alone made you top dog, he would have been it. Unfortunately, being top rooster in a flock required superlative skill and character. It takes size, strength and the boldness necessary to challenge other potential threats. The beauty of the rooster just comes with creation. But the drive to reach the top comes from the individual. A package deal is a must.

Puffing out his feathers and crowing certainly seemed to do the job, but the hens insisted that they needed more than that. They wanted the real deal. This eye candy came to maturity right alongside the other rooster I had in the flock. But while both were the same age and had the same reproductive ability, there grew to be a startling difference in the way the hens related to one rooster over the other. While the second rooster's plumage was rooster-worthy, he was not at all as delightful to see, but he was top rooster! He was proud and stately. He walked with confidence. He protected and herded, and he earned his place. Watching him rise to dignitary was enlightening, but his rise was the silkie's fall. That poor silkie found no peace in that coop. Not only did he have daily rivalry with the top rooster, the hens even challenged him. His " manhood" slowly disappeared. In a very short period of time, he had to be removed. We found him living in the corner.

He was no longer able to even be trusted by us, his caretakers. His placement in the flock, or *displacement,* caused him to act out abuse and immaturity. He could no longer be a protector. He confused dominance with leadership. He became useless to the farm. He wasn't even able to be given his own flock because he was damaged. He was culled from the flock and allowed to free range and look pretty on the farm. It kept him alive, but definitely not the kind of life a rooster was born to live. The question was posed: "What does a rooster do when his role has been taken away?" The answer: He becomes damaged, sometimes useless. This is a hard word, but truth.

Your design dictates your use or usefulness. If you were designed to be a rooster, then your usefulness is in your ability to function as a rooster without a vacancy in the role. There's no possibility for functionality in the role. Subsequently, he won't thrive in your home, nor would he be any good in any other, until and without divine intervention.

Does it matter who takes his place or why? What if it's his wife, because he keeps messing up? The answer is still NO. Whatever reason feels rational to absolve your husband of his role as "man" in your life is a big mistake! It keeps you from your greatest expression of womanhood, and you jettison his ability to become the man you want him to be. Demotion will only further the disruption in the home.

I'll tell you this, the equilibrium in the henhouse never was so balanced as when that silkie was removed and the strong rooster played his role. Everyone felt secure. The hens freely roamed about as the rooster confidently followed and protected, never feeling competition from the hens. The hens seemed happy and complacent to be hens. Peace had ensued.

I now know that same peace. I have never felt so free to flourish in my role as a woman since I found peace in walking through life by my hubby's side. I am able to freely roam about, being and doing what I feel called to do, while he confidently follows and leads and always protects. I couldn't rest if I was trying to compete. There would be a perpetual urge to do it all, to know all and be all. I know that my strength comes from yielding. My peace comes from being protected, and my freedom of flight comes from being covered. It didn't come without some pitfalls along the way. There were times he led without maturity and grace, and times he followed for lack of concern. But by us both finding our place and allowing the other to live theirs, we have created a house of triumph. Coming to the understanding of God's perfect design led us to a place of intimacy. We've raised boys who cherish and love me like he does. He set the stage for them to embrace leadership by strength of character and a firm confidence in allowing their future wives a growth plate of dimensions. Our daughters will, God willing, grow to be strong and capable without the need to ride the competition wave for leadership. They will find solace in staying women.

The truth is … we can't do it all! We were never created to be in competition with men, especially our lovers. We were never designed to perform the tasks of fathers, though often forced to raise children without them. Thank God, He can be a father to the fatherless and give women the ability to do what they have to do like Lois, Timothy's mother, whether the men in their lives are in the home and not being the men God called them to be, or are not around at all. Women will live the truest expression of womanhood when they are free to actually be women. That doesn't mean nanny, housekeeper, etc., although she may "do" many of those things. Our jobs don't define who we are.... our designs do.

I know that there are things that happen in relationships that set into motion a series of events that lead up to gender/role chaos in relationships. But it never really was meant to be. I have seen couples who have run into problems because the woman makes more money than the man. Situations get stressed when the woman is better than the husband at handling the finances. Some men are better at cooking or caring for the children than women. These examples are the reasons why some relationships experience drama around identities. Associating the role with the identity of an individual can be a set-up for disaster. I am a woman not because I cook, clean or fill what is thought of as a "feminine role," I am a woman because that is what God has destined and designed me to be. I am a strong woman, not because I'm in control or wear the pants. Quite the contrary. I am a strong woman because I play the part God created me to play. I am equipped and designed to accompany and walk in harmony with "man." My man.

Ladies, don't let the enemy hijack our love stories by inciting us to battle. He has created a crafty mess, both in the body of Christ and in the world. Remember the start of the book. If you remember who you are, then you won't get mixed up in fighting for what's already yours. God intended you to be a helpmate. So help. That's not ungodly. He equipped you to lead, rule and walk in dominion. That command was given to both. Again, there was no gender battle in the garden. They had a perfect love, uncorrupted by sin, untainted by demonic influence to compete. So for us to infer our fears in the union of co-dominion is to deny what God structured. Let me state for the record that I do believe that my husband is the head! But let me also state that the down-playing of the woman's part in the significance of creation is evil. We are important to the overall health and well-being in all areas. Can you imagine the world without women? Can you imagine your home without you? Imagine what your husband would be like today if it weren't for you.

I heard a funny story about a guy who had become mayor. He and his wife were riding on a float in a parade. They passed a mechanic shop along the way, and while waving at the crowds, the mayor saw his wife's ex-boyfriend, who was the mechanic.

With a smile on his face, proud as he could be, he turned to his wife and said, "Aren't you glad you married me? Otherwise you'd be the wife of a mechanic."

She, with the same cute smile, responded, "If I would have married him, he would have been the mayor."

In other words, she believed she was responsible for encouraging him to be all he could be. We are helpers. We do aid, as well as lead sometimes. We are strong enough to battle, but also strong enough to yield to the man we choose to walk life out with. You choose him. The Bible admonishes women to submit to "their own husbands." You choose the man you must submit to.

I could sum it up this way: Strong women are not strong because they are driven to compete with men. We are strong because we are capable of standing alone, yet strong enough to stand beside. Choose well. While on the issue of choice, let me say to the single ladies who have not yet chosen, your strength definitely lies within your choice. Choose a man who is capable of walking alongside a strong woman who knows her value. Make sure he is capable of being committed to growth himself. Be discriminating about your choice. Not every man with a job is eligible to lead you. He needs to complement you and complement the level of life you are called to.

Let me explain. If you want to lead a group on purity and you choose to live your life with a man who struggles with sexual improprieties, there will be a disconnect. Your ability to lead that group will be greatly stifled. But if you choose well, you will virtually be able to chart your own course. Nothing will be impossible for two people who love each other and speak the same language, united in covenant.

Does this sound amazing? Watch this. In Genesis, there is a story of a group of people building the Tower of Babel. Now, this was not a "God thing" to build this tower, but this is what God said about their unity. The LORD said, *"If as one people speaking the same language they have begun to do this, then nothing they plan to do will be impossible for them."* Genesis 11:6 Powerful. Then he goes on to say this: *"Come, let Us go down and there confuse their language, so that they will not understand one another's speech."* Genesis 11:7 The power you have to choose right is vital to your calling and success.

Without the right union, and same language, nothing you attempt to do will work, because you will not be speaking the same language. There will be a disconnect that will cease any and all progress. I can't stress enough this power you have in choice.

I believe that God is raising up women in all areas to dispel the lies the enemy has sold us, and to speak hope again, where once it was lost. To realign the walking together of the two that have become one, both identities are needed. Both were part of the grand design. To demote or decrease the importance of either is to go against what God Himself said is good. He brought Adam Eve because Adam needed Eve. Likewise, Eve needed Adam. The mess began when they acted exclusive of one another.

Ladies, speak up. Be the women God called you to be. Find your place in society, the church, and your home. Be a woman, feminine and beautiful, yet full of strength, valor and wisdom. Strong and alone is weak. To celebrate strength that seeks to dominate is just misguided. There needs to be grace in leadership and trust in following, recognizing that God designed both man and woman for tandem dominion.

5

Life Uncluttered

C lutter is defined as a collection of things lying about in an untidy mass. Do you have clutter in your life? Are you going through life with collections of things lying about in your heart, mind and soul in untidy masses?

Several years ago God began to ask me to "clean my house." Actually, He used the word "declutter." I set out on a journey to begin to set up a schedule for the year to declutter my home and barns. Little did I know that as I began this quest, I would find that God was not only seeing behind the door of my home, He was looking into the den of my heart. Boy, did I have clutter. Every hurt and disappointment of the past was resting right there behind closet doors set up to neatly close out the masses from guests.

Of course we all have clutter, we just learn to live with it. What's the big deal? Clutter prevents us from seeing clearly, loving clearly, and even hearing clearly. Everything that comes into our lives and leaves our mouths is filtered through our hearts, and if your heart is clogged with an untidy mass, everything that comes from there will come from and through untidiness.

"Keep thy heart with all diligence; for out of it are the issues of life." **Proverbs 4:23** This verse confirmed my mess and my need to address the mess. Out of the heart flow the issues of life. Man, were there issues of life that had become cluttered and complicated. There were things I had suppressed and shoved deep into the closet of my heart that would prove to hinder God's purpose for my life. My ability to love, my ability to let things go, the speed at which I was able to deal with offense. It was all cluttered. Right, wrong...even why when things happened. I had clutter from past events where I couldn't even remember the details of the story. Yet the garbage was still there.

God had to get me into those cluttered places to show me just how fragmented I was, and the smallness of my perception. My soul had begun to speak to me from the perspective of the circumstances, and I believed them. The problem with that is that depending on where we stand, our perspective can be limited. God has to now clear the view to bring us to a place that we see life from His perspective.

Abraham experienced this when he received a promise from God that he would be the father of nations. Well, when you have no children and you desperately want one — he and Sarah both getting on in years and seemingly nothing was happening — not only is it difficult to believe what you can't see, you have also now made an even bigger mess of your life. Broken and down on hope, this was how God dealt with Abraham.

> **Genesis 15:4-6** reads... *"4 Then behold, the word of the LORD came to him, saying, 'This man will not be your heir; but one who will come forth from your own body, he shall be your heir.' And He took him outside and said, 'Now*

look toward the heavens, and count the stars,

if you are able to count them.' And He said to

him, 'So shall your descendants be.' 6Then he

believed in the LORD; and He reckoned it to

him as righteousness...Then he believed God..."

Isn't it just like God to know exactly what would be needed for Abraham to believe? Nothing in the natural had changed. Abraham was still only holding onto words. So what was it about this encounter with the Lord that would change the way Abraham would see things? What would cause him to "now" believe God? God bringing Abraham outside and saying, "Look,count the stars." In other words: Look at something differently than what you have been focused on. He changed Abraham's perspective, and perspective caused hope to rise.

Have you ever been at a place where you became cluttered with the emotions that arise from waiting on God and living with the Ishmael you created? Every circumstance surrounding the issue of Ishmael created clutter in the lives of Abraham and Sarah. Clutter that prevented them from moving forward into destiny, until God caused Abraham to look at the situation from a different angle.

Remember, I mentioned in earlier chapters the fact that the journey of life was meant to grow us into the person that was big enough to carry the promise? Clutter compromises the journey, placing every hurdle in your life into opposition to your growth. Offenses and particles that we carry from past hurts and situations of life make our hearts heavy, unforgiving and bitter. Bitterness creeps in where we least expect it, locked far into the closet of our hearts. It corrupts and taints the way we think and dream. It inhibits our ability to hope for something new. Behold, God makes all things new! But for you, you won't be able to see the new. Fifteen years ago this thing happened and you're still feeling the same anger you felt when it originally occurred. At any moment you could cry the same tears you shed ten years earlier.

I heard TD Jakes say, "God will promote you to the level of your tolerance to pain." Big people allow pain to propel them into their purpose. Luke 12:48 reads, "to whom much is given, much is required." "Or much is required of whom much is given." If we want to be women who do exploits for God, living uncluttered is a must! We have to learn to turn tragedy into motion. Jakes also says, "If you can't handle it, you can't have it." It is vital to our existence to declutter. Become like ducks, where the issues of life, the pains of life, and the offenses of life run off our backs like water off a duck's back.

The uncluttered woman, is the woman who is determined to always be bigger than the challenges that accompany the journey. She is capable of encountering drama and pain without allowing it to mar her image, change her destiny and disposition.

One day in the pursuit of knowledge, Peter came to Jesus ... **Mathew 18:21-22** *"21Then Peter came and said to Him, 'Lord, how often shall my brother sin against me and I forgive him? Up to seven times?' 22Jesus said to him, 'I do not say to you, up to seven times, but up to seventy times seven.'"* Jesus was not trying to give a math lesson, he was trying to get Peter to see that there is no limit to the amount of times you must extend forgiveness. I'll admit I have asked God the same question. Lord, how many times do I have to be the one to forgive? How many times, Lord, do I have to be the one to get over it? How many times, Lord, do I have to be the one to suffer long and keep being kind?

We all go through those moments that we feel the pain of releasing someone from the pain they caused us. But letting go never means that we have to pretend to forget what happened. We just choose to rise above it. We choose to be bigger. Because we understand that not forgiving only hurts us.

I remember counseling a beautiful woman who went through some terrible issues with her husband. We'll call her Mary. Mary was sure that by insulating her heart, she would protect herself from ever being hurt or made a fool of again. Mary was living her life so defensively that every person in her life was struggling to penetrate the borders. Her children suffered, her marriage was obviously over, and her siblings were frustrated with the tones of their relationship. When we spoke the last time, she had decided that her unforgiveness had made her hard, and she celebrated that. "No will ever hurt me again, especially him." I remember feeling an overwhelming sense of remorse because there was no breaking through to her. I told her, "Your hands are clinched so tight to fight, and yes you are always ready for battle. But while your fists remain closed, you prevent anything else from getting into those hands. God Himself will not and cannot bless what you close off from Him."

Mary represents so many women. Things happened in our childhood, things have happened in our marriages, and things that we wish happened never did. As a result, we find solace in hiding amongst the clutter of our soul.

There's a story of a woman in the Bible called Michal. She was married to David. The only woman the Bible mentions, "loved her husband ." Not at all overplaying this phrase, as if to imply that other women didn't love theirs. But I believe it bears relevance in the tragic ending of this love story. Michal is an example of a woman who didn't understand how fearfully and wonderfully God made "her," a woman who was used as a pawn on the hands of her father and the man she loved. If that isn't enough to cause you to feel ugly, I'm not sure what would.

On a desperate quest for acceptance, she was a woman in years, but inside just a little girl dreaming of being loved. Michal arrived in the arms of a man she could never have imagined would be hers. A man destined to be king, a man who would be nobility and possess great wealth. David would receive Michal only after he would deliver the foreskins of 100 Philistine warriors to her father, the king. Since that was such a monumental task, Saul never imagined David would survive this endeavor and earn his daughter. But David would leap over this hurdle, and instead of bringing back 100 foreskins, he brought back 200. David won his bride and proved he was a valiant warrior. Valiant he was, but in love ... not so much.

One evening, Saul planned to kill David in his room while sleeping. Michal helped David escape and ensured her husband would one day be king. When her father learned of her betrayal, he was angry, but Michael would flat out told him,"You gave him to me as my husband," and blamed David as an excuse to calm the blow. Her father made one last attempt to block David's claim to the throne and gave his daughter to another man.

After Saul died, David would return to retrieve his wife. Not because he loved her, but because she strengthened his tie to the throne. Palteil actually really loved Michal and followed behind them, weeping until one of David's men made him turn back. One day while David was overcome with worship while bringing back the ark of the covenant, he began dancing down the street in nothing more than an ephod. Which was a priestly apron that only chief priests were allowed to wear . Michal watched from the windows in the palace, seething with anger, aghast at the common way that he would parade down the street. He exacerbated the blow by dancing right out of his clothes. There he was naked, and unashamed, freely dancing in ecstasy. Women and men alike were watching. This was more than she could take. When David came up to the room, she rebuked him, accusing him of showing off before the women.

So dishonored by the lack of understanding and pettiness on her part, David responded with the final blow of their marriage. He explained that his dancing was not vulgarity but worship. He went on to tell her that as king over all Israel, he would esteem himself even lower and dance before the Lord even more. He said these words that would show his lack of respect for her: "But among these slave girls you speak of… I will be honored." 2 Samuel 6:22 In other words, David was telling her that it was more palatable for him to have the attention of his servants rather than the respect of his royal wife. How humiliating this had to be for her. After all the sacrifices she had made. After being loved by Palteil and taken away to live a life of royal security without being loved.

She was ruined for love. Michal was never referred to again as David's wife. She was not noted among the list of David's wives. She was simple referred to as Saul's daughter. No sons, no story beyond tragedy. Just misfortune. I'm not sure Michal ever had a chance to really feel love. I wonder if she had a chance to enjoy the feeling of being honored by Palteil for that short time. But the man she loved and risked everything for never loved her. Her father used her and gave her away.

Michal had a story very much like many ladies today. Looking for love in all the wrong places. Choosing and devoted to the wrong man. Not appreciating the right man. Unable to receive love when it does come along. Perpetual seeking from men what we by design already possess. I wonder what the story would have looked like if, in the face of all the betrayal and hurt, she would have danced herself. What if she knew her value in God? What if she never allowed herself to be shuffled around and used as leverage in a game of war?

One of the most heartbreaking revelations of this story is that apart from her outbursts of anger at the man she loved, Michal gave no impression of her feelings throughout the whole story. Tugged and pulled from father to husband, then husband to husband, and yet no words. What clutter! Such a mess of emotions and reactions. How do you experience such degradation and not say a word? **2 Timothy 3:6-8** reads, *"For of this sort are those who creep into households and make captives of gullible women loaded down with sins, led away by various lusts, 7 always learning and never able to come to the knowledge of the truth."* Wow, this is powerful. When you are loaded down with sins hidden in your heart, led by your emotions due to issues, you haven't cleaned up in your heart's closet. You become gullible and cluttered to the point of vulnerability, easily used and abused, never insisting on being handled like a treasure, because you don't know you're a treasure. Love has no choice but to become distorted.

But notice the stark contrast between Michal's heart and the **Psalm 139:14** passage. *"I will praise You, for I am fearfully and wonderfully made; Marvelous are Your works, And that my soul knows very well."* David's song of self-understanding.

This heart is bathed in confidence. It can give love, receive love, and nurture love. This is the heart of a woman who understands who she is in God, and what she was created for. She could never be satisfied with a relationship of constant betrayal and would never find peace in being mistreated or devalued. She understands that her Father in heaven dances over her, and would insist that the man worthy of her love would dance over her too. She finds acceptance in the arms of God, who says that, *"he gathers his children together like a hen gathers her chicks."* Luke 13:34 and she would demand that the man who is in a relationship with her would protect her the same way. Her life praises God because she knows she is fearfully and wonderfully made. The most beautiful woman is the woman who is dressed in worth, clothed in confidence and uncluttered. She radiates the glory of God.

6.

Focus On The Fixtures...

I feel pretty, oh so pretty Remember that song from West side story written by Stephen Sondheim ? Corny as it is ...I couldn't help but start this chapter by quoting these amazing lyrics . When I sing it, I end up twirling around in front of my mirror in full actress mode. I hear Julie Andrews singing it and how could you help not to sing along when you hear this? This kind of beauty is not found in a dress size or a fashion frenzy. It's not given to you by plastic surgeons or *Vogue* magazine. It's found in the awareness of who I am and whose I am that makes me feel pretty. It's knowing the importance of what that feeling does for me that keeps me pursuing it. It's the need to feel that twirl, singing "I feel pretty" and the feeling that motivates.

Beauty and confidence is born when a woman becomes aware of what makes her feel good about herself. When she taps into that, she walks with a spring in her step and a joy in her being that radiates to everyone around her. Unfortunately, I had to find that out in my forties. After years of trying to keep up with the in style, though tailored to my liking, it was still somewhat dictated by someone else's standard of beauty. Why do we buy that stuff? Why do we wiggle and struggle to fit into an image in an industry's mind of what is beautiful? It's limited, to say the least. The image and standard of beauty is as vast as there are humans.

So ladies, let this be the day of liberty. Find your description of beauty and embody it. You will never be more successful than when you find what makes you feel pretty and capture it. You will never be more alluring to others than when you find that place of inward glow. She shines for the world to see. She devastates goals and leaps over challenges. She becomes unrestrained by life's complications, and uninhibited by cheap male perverted images of body structure. She makes the rules and does not bow to them. She finds the joy of eating and laughing because she is not afraid of a calorie or a carb. She is woman. Can you hear her roar?

Women, for far too long, have been so boxed. so molded. Can we please be what we were created by God to be? Not allowing ourselves to be recreated in this life by humans. God has made us fearfully and wonderfully. Meaning He, in an anxious manner, took His time to design me just the way I am. And He did it well, with all my shortcomings, with all my insecurities, with all my seeming faults. God, the creator of the universe, took the focused time to make me. He said, "It is good!" What could make you feel more wonderful, more pretty? When you know that, you will take great offense to an industry or individual trying to squeeze you into a makeover machine. Be the best you that you were created to be. When you find what makes you feel beautiful, run with it.

When you feel beautiful, you live beautifully. When you are in shape and energized, you have the strength to run the race of life. When you feel sexy, you become the "woman," not just a mother. If you just gasped because I said sexy, and weren't sure you read that right. You did. I said it: be sexy!

Scripture has commanded women to "dress decently and in order," and to be modest in our apparel. The problem with that is that there is a lot of false representation of what the word of God would seem to portray to us about dress.

1 Timothy 2:9 says, *"Likewise, I want women to adorn themselves with proper clothing, modestly and discreetly, not with braided hair and gold or pearls or costly garments."* Scripture is warning against the high price paid for clothing that women were spending for their attire and fashion over the investment into their spiritual maturity. It was an admonishment to properly balance out the place you give to fashion and the adornment of the outward man. To rightly divide beautifying the flesh and the character of the imagebaring saint.

We see this plainly spoken in the very next verse: *"but rather by means of good works, as is proper for women making a claim to godliness."* As a woman who makes a claim to "godliness," her claim should be reflected in her character. She should look like a God follower, not JUST a fashion follower.

Let not adorning be simply in the external. I am not condemning adorning in and of itself. God never said, "Ladies, please dress ugly, stop combing your hair and it probably would be a good idea if you didn't brush your teeth either." Forgive me for being facetious.

Now that we have cleared the air on the issue about what scripture has to say about "modesty," I think it apropos to define modesty. Modesty is "behavior, manner, or appearance intended to avoid impropriety or indecency." Modesty has become what looks like: a style, rather than simply what God said it was. Avoid impropriety in dress. Modesty has become a "style" amongst some groups. Ironically, even within them, they argue about how long their skirts and sleeves on the T-shirt should be. When humans starts trying to use God's principles to exploit their agenda, there will always be hypocrisy. Modest is not synonymous with plain, and your style neither cures nor causes lust in the hearts of people. The command to be modest was a command for all people who represent the kingdom to be properly dressed and clothed with the grace becoming of a child of the King.

Early on in my homeschooling, I was looking for cama-
raderie and support as a new homeschooling mom. I joined
a homeschool group like every good homeschool mom does.
Our first field trip was to a farm. Excited as I was about this
adventure, as I too was dreaming of being a farmer myself. I
set out to meet a large group of women who were likeminded
and sold out to raise godly children and be good wives. I got
my crew dressed, ready for the day. We arrived at the farm
full of expectation. What I got was shunned! Come on, ladies.
My cream colored corduroy overalls weren't modest enough?
According to the group of ladies I found myself with, corduroy
in the form of pants was taboo. I stood off by myself with my
children, feeling very alone and condemned. It was as if I were
standing there, scantily clad in a red dress with the sign hanging
over my head, "JEZEBEL."

It wasn't enough to shun me — they stood in a circle,
talking loudly enough for me to hear about my attire. They
proceeded to talk about "how some people were condoning
skirts that they felt were too short ." I'm not sure what Bible
they read that morning before they set off to go to the farm,

but the Bible I read says that we should love one another. I assume that the spiritual job of playing the Holy Spirit fashion police was more important than that particular scripture, and God was more concerned about my pants than hearts. Ladies, come on. I'm wondering how much of this behavior hinges on the fear that if our husbands actually saw the form of another woman, they would stray? Can I send you back to **Mark 7:15**: *"Nothing outside a person can defile them by going into them. Rather, it is what comes out of a person that defiles them."* Our husbands and sons are not kept holy by controlling the community around them. They are kept by a Holy Spirit invasion of the heart.

Trust me, I'm fully aware of the reprehensible lack of clothing we see as a trend today. In no way am I saying that sexuality in front of our children doesn't damage them. Neither am I making a case for pornography. God did instruct us to be careful not to increase the chance of someone sinning. I'm pretty sure overalls wouldn't do that.

A precious women I met years ago was a homeschool mom, sweet as can be. When I first met her, she wore her beautiful hair in a bun every day, wore jean skirts every day with a T-shirt, and no makeup. After about three years had passed, I saw her again, only this time she had a cute little haircut, exposing her wonderful locks. She had a nice outfit on, a pair of shorts, actually, and had makeup on her face. While we were talking, I couldn't get over how beautiful she looked, and all the while I was wondering, what was the change? She spoke of how she had gotten training to be a fitness instructor and loved it, and how sadly her husband had an affair with a blond bombshell and was happily with her still. Knowing that it would never come out right, I didn't have the heart to ask her if her husband had seen her lately.

Please don't get the impression that I think that husbands won't cheat if we stay marketable. I know they do!!! But here's my point. It's not about him! It's about her, you, and all of us. Women in particular tend to internalize everything. Everything that comes into our lives stands the chance to either affect or infect our lives. Betrayal always hurts and requires time to heal. Adding regret to the list of things to be healed is not necessary. Holding on to your confidence that you lived your marriage and life, proud of the way you respected yourself and your person can only help. God is not asking us to look plain, to hide our femininity and let ourselves go. Our husbands live in a world where beauty is pursued, where fashion has become how little clothing you can possibly get away with. While that is not what God's people should partake of , we certainly can't forget to focus on the fixtures.

Ladies, your husbands need to see you looking presentable at least a great portion of the time. You need to remember to keep up with you first for you. Where's the woman you were before you were a mother? Under all that flour and house-cleaning supplies? Behind that desire to keep home and tend to our children is a woman who needs to be expressed. Let her shine! You'll be a better mom and wife for it. If then he still chooses to stray, you won't be left wondering: Did I perhaps neglect or abandon me? Did I forget to "stay womanly"?

Why did this precious woman find herself after her husband left her for another woman? I have no idea whatever became of that couple or her. I'm fairly sure that she will stumble upon some great-looking guy who will hopefully give her the world. Let not your adorning be simply be in your appearance, meaning adorn yourself, just not only the outward aspect of yourself. Both inward and outward are necessary. Both make a complete woman.

If you feel that God has challenged you to wear skirts, then do that. But in doing so, remember to remain feminine in the process. It sends a message to the world, your children and your husband. Speak well of yourself. Remember that before anyone will ever read your pages, they will see the book cover.

Is it okay to be sexy? RESOUNDING YES!!!!! Please be sexy!! Just not every day, not at the soccer game with Johnny. But there is a place for you to be sexy. Women are created with curves and lumps that were not just made for the mechanics of childbirth and reproduction. I'm sure God could have made milking machines without such brilliance that would have been efficient enough to simply feed our babies. He creatively and wonderfully created the female body with beauty beyond reproduction. In a society that has discounted the need for curves and a little plumpness, let me take this moment to say that breasts and booties are made of fatty tissue. You might want to reconsider how much of that you want to curse, Just saying.

On a serious note: Ladies, it's not a sin to dress sexy for your husband. God is not going to be displeased with you if you go buy a sexy dress for date night. Live a little, lighten up and explore sexy for you. It may not be the sexy your girlfriend is comfortable with, but it's your level of sexy.

Make your husband sit across the table and wonder the entire evening. Not about the bills he has to pay, not about what the kids are going to do next or how he's going to get through the next work day. Make him completely focused on how beautiful his wife is. Make him remember what it was like to date you and feel the challenge of other men noticing his beautiful wife. That man should be wondering one thing: Is he going to get lucky tonight? Your date night dress does not have to be expensive. I have found several at Goodwill. It has to be fun, it has to be "date night worthy," and has to reflect the image you want to portray. Flirty and feminine.

Some of the greatest fun I had with my husband was an occasion we went out on a date. We left the kids and farm behind. I had a cute black dress that flowed in the wind like

Marilyn Monroe. When I came down the steps, I saw my husband's face and I knew: "touchdown." He was excited to be my husband. He was proud of his wife. And I was so proud of him. It's amazing how a dress can change the atmosphere. I had definitely set the tone for the night. From the start there was something a little extra special about that night. We were in the car and our conversation was about how each other looked. We laughed and told jokes. We took a few stops down memory lane and kept on driving. The entire evening was filled with smiles and pride. We were in love with the fact that after all these years, we still had the fire. We were in love with our love. Twelve kids and nine horses hadn't knocked the cool out of us, and we were in awe of how that felt.

We went dancing after dinner, and for the first time in a long time, morning found us exhausted. What a night to remember. I was convinced that that $8 dress was the match that struck the flame. Yeah, I was in it. But it was the dress that made me feel pretty sexy. It was the dress that kicked it up a notch. The dress reminded me, I'm a woman. That night I wasn't mom. I wasn't a housekeeper. Just woman. The lesson was clear. Sexy was okay. God smiled on us.

We keep the spark alive and I surprise my husband quite frequently with similar dresses. Not always sexy. But always special. I'll admit that over the years, it seemed more "holy" to be plain. I leaned on the fact that my husband is faithful and I didn't need to do all that. Conflicted by being a woman and being a godly woman, I was confused. But God in His infinite mercy allowed me to happen upon that black dress that woke me up. They were one and the same. Godly women can get creative with their attire. They can be concerned with the exterior of the house *and* the interior. They can host the presence of the Lord and look good while they do it. They can be led by His Spirit to be sure they never go too far.

The divorce rate even amongst evangelicals is still higher than we care to say. While it is getting better, we still have a lot of work to do to save our Christian homes. I read a recent report that stated that being a Conservative Protestant increased your chances of divorce. How sad! I'm wondering how much of that hinges on us perpetuating silly arguments about right and wrong that the Bible never said.

Without getting stuck out on a bunny trail, I'm going to journey right to where I want to leave you. You can be a very modest, conservative Bible believing Christian woman, yet full of spunk and wonder with your husband. There is a place and time for everything. You may not want to wear that dress you buy for date night to Sunday service. Please don't! But girl-friend, neither do you need to wear that Sunday service dress out on a date with your hubby! Go buy a sexy black dress and plan a date with your hubby. You are a woman! Don't get stuck on the tragic notion that you stopped being a woman when you became a mother and wife. If you're still single, stay pure and pretty. Take this lesson into your marriage. When you meet the man of your dreams, remind him often of what he got when he found you.

Years ago when my kids were younger, I used to go about the majority of my week in my pajamas. I woke up and cleaned the house, bathed my kids and did all that I needed to do around the house. I saw no need to get dressed as I wasn't going anywhere, and to put clothes on seemed to only add to the large laundry pile. I'm embarrassed to say that went on for years. I did, however, elevate into sweat pants here and there. My husband is such a trooper because he never said a word. He came home every day, kissed my forehead, and still told me I was the most beautiful woman in the world to him. I believe he meant it.

One day when I got the urge to put some clothes on and some make up, I stood in the doorway of my room and one of my children came by and said, "Mom, where are you going?" It was as if a mountain fell on me. All at once I realized the example I set for my children. They thought I only got dressed when I was going someplace. And in those days that was Sunday to Sunday for church. I vowed to myself to never allow myself to go there again. Every day was worth the greeting of expectation. Whether I was going out or not, my husband and children deserved to get the best me I could give them. When you get dressed, you feel better about yourself. You smile a little more. You glow and you walk a little sassier. I want my children to grow up with a healthy perspective on taking care of themselves. I want them to know that it's more than okay to take care of yourself. Focusing on the fixture is part of that.

As I started taking that approach to my day, I found that I began to grow. Believe it or not, it started with getting up and getting dressed every day. It helped me to remember who I was. And my husband got his woman back. Every date night, we both honor each other by getting dressed for a date, like it was our first date. God designed us to feel good when we take the time to invest in ourselves. It's a worthwhile endeavor. It really is acknowledging the fact that I am worth it. Just for me. So work out. Get that membership to the gym, if you need to. Start walking the block. Make sure that you invest the time you need to feel pretty and confident, so that you can be the woman God called you to be. Be careful not to start comparing yourself to the industry's level of beauty. That would be a disaster. You don't need plastic surgery or a whole new wardrobe. Just take the mirror and focus it on you, the housing of the great woman who resides inside.

Feminine is elegance. The definition: having qualities or appearance traditionally associated with women, especially delicate and pretty. Some synonyms are: womanly, ladylike, girlish, soft. Don't you just feel pretty hearing those words? The artistry of woman is feminine. Don't be afraid to let her shine. She is carefully designed. Elegant woman. So go ahead. Focus on your fixtures a bit. Find that you're beautiful and let her out. You'll know her when you find her. She'll be twirling around in the mirror, singing, "I feel pretty."

7.

Me In The Mess...

B aby puke, nursing, cleaning the house and laundry: how do you expect me to take care of me when all I do is take care of everyone else? Isn't that what I'm here for? To sacrifice, to die to self, to hold it all together?

I know the feeling. Trust me, I've been there. You get up in the morning, put the coffee on, and usher your husband off to work refreshed and clean. The night before, you maybe pulled in a couple of hours of sleep, but nothing significant to speak of. You're tired but you know what the day has in store for you, and there's no room for tired in your vocabulary. You start the laundry as the kids begin to trickle down the stairs...oh no, I woke someone up. One by one, you start the breakfast cafe and while you're doing that, dinner pops in your mind and you must think about what to pull out of the freezer, realizing you forgot to do it the night before. Before you could finish the first rush of breakfast, the baby is crying and now you have to stop what you're doing to sit down and nurse him. As resourceful as you are, you figure out a way to nurse and make the oatmeal. Off to play the balancing act. Baby on the right boob and the left hand (not my hand of strength) stirring the oatmeal.

I'm thinking now that I forgot to pour my own cup of coffee. Wait, I did, but I left it on the table and now it's cold. I run to the coffee maker to pour another cup, when now there has erupted upstairs a fight between the girls that is so loud the baby that was so close to going back to sleep is now wide awake. Annoyed and frustrated that I can't just get a cup of coffee in me and the world is now in need of me, it's barely 10am and I'm already asking Calgon to take me away. Before long, peace seems to fill the halls of my house, and just as I think I love my life, it's time to get dinner underway. Ugh, I thought about it but never really took anything out of the freezer. Now I must get creative and make ….mystery casserole. I pretend like I got this recipe off Pinterest rather than admit it, the brain child of a twist between what was in the cabinet and what was left in the fridge. Because my crew is gracious, they loved the casserole and now I'm cleaning the kitchen. Believe it or not, it is actually a very peaceful time of the day, as no one wants to hang around too long in the kitchen for fear they may be asked to do some work.

Kitchen cleaned, the laundry needs to be switched, and the bedtime story needs to be read. Hubby tries to read the story but he doesn't add the crazy voices like I do, so the kiddies want Mom instead. I read with the last bit of energy I can muster up, with of course the baby on the boob AGAIN… and then, thank God, it's lights out…for the kids. I turn another load in the washer, pick up a few toys so the next day doesn't start out an absolute mess, then I head up to bed. Seriously, NOW my husband has needs!!! Somebody, please give me a break.

Sound familiar? Or at least some resemblance to familiar? Add horses, goats, a pig and twelve kids to that day, and you can feel me.

If there is anyone capable of talking about not losing "me" in the course of life and the daily shuffle? It's me. I learned a long time ago that no one is going to "give" you the break you need. No one is going to hand you that pause button you so desperately seek. You are going to have to make up in your mind that you will hit the pause button for yourself. If you're anything like me, you can find a million reasons why the world would fall apart if you weren't there, if you didn't do what you did, if you didn't cook dinner, if you didn't wash the clothes today, if you didn't play caretaker to the child who is an addict, if you didn't take care of your parents alongside taking care your kids, if you didn't coach your husband when he feels like he hates his job and wants to run and hide. Or the girlfriend whose marriage is on the rocks. If you didn't call and wake up that child who moved out last year.. If you didn't host that group the church needs you to hold.

The madness goes on. The truth is, more often than not, the reasons we tell ourselves that we can do it all is because at the center of it all, we are so fragmented that there is something in that mess that feels oddly safe. It's all you know. Who else will do it? We get so accustomed to living fragmented that we have no idea what it's like to be whole. A piece of me here, a piece of me there, and all I know is that I value the pieces that I'm giving away so much that I fear "what would happen if those pieces were no longer available," even if for a day. There's a comfort in believing I am the link that holds it all together. I thought the fragmenting would get better, the older the kids got, the more life I lived. But all that happened was the fragmenting got worst.

I knew I wasn't alone in this because I talked to women. I watched women young and old. And what I saw was a whole lot of women who had lost themselves, with no idea of how to find themselves amongst the scattered pieces. How do you even begin to put those pieces back together again? How do you find the time to be a daughter of the king when your own daughter is dating a jerk and she needs you to focus on her? How could I dream when I was way too involved in helping my kids chase their dreams? Where was "me in the mess" of life? Who is that person anymore, anyway? I started out with dreams, plans and desires for my family and my own life. But somewhere I just started in motion, just doing things. Seasons were changing around me and I just moved with wind, tossed to and fro "By every wind of doctrine." Life and issues dictated what I did, the direction I moved. Not vision.

The pressure builds. I started lashing out, knowing it's the build-up that's worst. I blame myself even more because I think I'm scarring my kids for life. I could travel around this way a bit longer and know that I would stumble on the path to where you live. But I think you've seen yourself somewhere in all this.

So let me take out the time to speak life into you. For this moment that you have taken the time out to invest in you, let's make this time worth the journey. The absolute best contribution you could make to your family, marriage, church or organization, is to be whole, confident, uncluttered and sure. Your confidence gets crushed every day that you make the decision to function fragmented. (Some of you aren't ever even on your priority list.) It absolutely requires confidence and peace of mind to make sound decisions, to find the strength to get up again and do what you do. Million dollar ideas, wisdom for your children, answers for your household, all come from vision. I know you have lost vision if you are not sure of who you are anymore, if you're so fragmented that you have lost "you" in the mess. Locked up inside this life, "you" built a life-style of deficit living. Nothing in, certainly nothing out!

Proverbs 29:18 says *"Where there is no vision,* the people perish." Well, perish means die. Where there is no vision, death begins to take over. What confidence do you have to believe that things will ever get better? Can you believe for better days? Can you find the drive to hope for a day when things are going to be easier, if you have stopped dreaming? If the vision you had for your marriage, your family and your ministry or company has fallen by the wayside in the course of life, then you are just a dead woman walking! No hope, no drive and no ambition. Traveling from one day to the next, doing what you're doing.

But there's hope if you feel this despair. There's a God-given purpose inside you that supersedes every season of life you're in. And that purpose is to "be" something. Not "do" something. If all you're doing is "doing" life, then you are dwelling carelessly. Situations, seasons and relationships change in life. What happens when they change? Do you cease to be relevant, important, or even necessary? No! Those are seasons! Things you do! Tell yourself every day: "This is subject to change." And change, it will. More than likely, you will still be here. The question you need to ask yourself is: When it does change? What will you be? What will you have left of you? God designed you for Him. To "be" something to Him. What you do in this season you're in doesn't change that. If your marriage fails, you are not a failure. Your marriage just failed. If you made a bad decision, you're not a terrible mother. You just made a bad choice. God called you to be in covenant relationship with Him, to lavish on you with His covenant promises and purpose. Everything that you do in this life is icing on the cake.

But if you allow yourself to get so caught up in the doing that you abandon that covenant, forget the you, that started it all. The covenant woman who is the key to the puzzle. You will struggle to find the strength to move forward. Do you know who she is? Have you lost yourself in the doing of life? Maybe lost yourself in a bad move you made while living exactly what I'm explaining? Is the expression of you just as fragmented as your thoughts and heart? One day you're strong and encouraged. The next day, weak and impotent. One day you're emotionally together. The next, challenged.

Life can be rough. Our husbands lose their minds. Our children flip out and forget every bit of teaching you sacrificed to put in them, and the unexpected things that appear challenge the best of us. Believe me, in those moments, that's not the time to lose you. Talk about regret. You will carry a life time of "what ifs" if you allow you to slip away in the mess.

As my kids got old enough to go out on their own, knowing I couldn't be all places to protect them and steer them away from bad choices, I would say to them every time they would leave the house. "Remember who you are." Taken straight from Mufassa in *The Lion King*. Sometimes we moms need to remind ourselves that. "Remember who you are." Call to mind the things God whispered in your ear during the daily grind. When faced with the temptation to give up on you, roar out. Remember who you are.

My dad shared a story with me that I call to memory frequently. He told me of a time when God asked him the question,

"What is a wise man?" After a day of walking, working and pondering the question, he imagined many answers. Some, I'm sure, were great. One his way home from work that day, God encountered him with the answer. He said, "A wise man is one who knows his limitations and remains within them." This is how I carry that profound statement. A wise, productive woman is the woman who knows who she is and whose she is. And no matter where life takes her, she remains aware of that knowledge.

I struggled for many years with that question. Who was I? I knew I was a mother. I was a wife, a pastor. I was a lot of things, wore a lot of hats. But who was "that woman." Before I was all those things …who was I? The question begged answers, because at some point those seasons were going to change. The dust was going to settle and I was going to need to get reacquainted with me. As a minister, I tried to define who I was. Was I a singer, a preacher, an inspirational speaker? The questions held me hostage to the expressions of my gifts . Nothing quite complete was coming out of me because I was still indebted by the quandary. I couldn't move confidently in the direction of my dreams when I wasn't quite sure what they were, or who I was. God had begun to minister to my heart. My dad and husband through the years told me, "You're more than just a singer." But what did that mean? I also knew I was more than just a mother, but what was that? Well the "me" in the mess of life came screaming at me one profound day. I remember that moment, not because it was some profound glorious lightning strike revelation. In fact, the simplicity of the occasion was humbling. I was just me!!! Just me. Yes, I did many things. 'Me" was expressed in many ways. But at the end of the day, still me.

That revelation helped me begin the process of picking up the pieces. Everything I did came through me. I was the minister. At any time the expression can change, but it didn't change who I was. I could function as a mom and wife, and those expressions were different but still pieces of me. It was abundantly clear to me that when my children left home, I would be an empty nester and my expression of motherhood would change, but nothing else. It all started to make sense to be me, the importance of this revelation. I needed to be aware of the pieces of me so I could express me. Everyone in my life who depended on me needed me, would only be satisfied if I maintained me in the mess.

I couldn't afford to live fragmented. I couldn't afford to lose "me in the mess." I couldn't allow life's business and issues to undermine the me that would determine how I would function, my unique approach to ministry and motherhood. My husband needed "me." The expression of me that attracted him to "me" in the first place. Not just the crazy woman who resented sex and date night because she was too busy and frazzled. Too down on myself because I let myself go and acquired an appearance that echoed it. My children needed me. The mom I was when I was sure of myself. Funny and energized. Excited about motherhood. Enjoying their company. "That me" the me only I could be.

One night while cleaning up in the barn, where I often go to find peace and my perspective, my older boys came up to see what I was doing. Spontaneous fun erupted as they began jumping off the loft into a pile of shavings. I laughed gut belly laughs with them. They flipped and twirled and were having so much fun. One of my boys yelled out, "Mom, try it!"

Really? Not! I watched from the sidelines for a while. Then all of a sudden this urge came over me. There was a time I would do that with no problem. So up the ladder I went. I walked to the edge and ... *I believe I can fly*. I jumped. What fun that turned out to be. The butterflies in my stomach and the feeling of adrenaline. Up again I went, to do it again.

The next night we returned for more of our homemade fun. Only this time my husband came along. Up the ladder again I went, but the pile looked a little smashed down. Hesitation came over me and this jump landed me at the bottom, ten feet down with a shattered ankle.

The coming days and weeks alloted me time that I wasn't used to having. Bored out of my mind at first, through sheer lack of anything else I could do, I started to think. Just think. Thinking about what life had become. How happy I was about so much that my kids had done. Thinking about how my husband's career had really turned out so successful. And really kind of seeing the role I'd played in the process of a lot of that. Yet, really hadn't completed much of what I started dreaming I'd be. One would argue that with giving birth to ten children and co-raising two others, that was about all I should have been worried about.

It would have been easier if that were the case, but there was something, some things more inside of me. I started listening to a podcast every day of faith-building messages, because I was challenged by a woman whose ministry really influenced me to change. I heard her say one day on a podcast, "you're either going to have excuses or results." That rocked my world. Sure, I had a lot on my plate. But I thought that the God who gave me all that knew that when He designed me, yet still He put these dreams in me. I started to consider how I am a champion for other people's dreams. I'm always encouraging and helping my children start businesses and chase their dreams. Yet I was doing little about my own, lost in the mix of life.

I personally think this is the reason we see so many parents fighting on soccer fields. They never accomplished their own hopes for the future, so they are determined to see their children do what they never did. Having children, growing older, or running into life obstacles were never meant to serve as a death sentence to your dreams. Daring to dream again, I knocked the dust off my journals and started to write again. In those pages I found a growing resolve to consider.

Could God be reminding me of who I was? Could He be giving me this time out to change my life? When I finally resumed my daily activities, I was armed with the knowledge that my family could do what I was so used to doing. Life would not fall apart if I took a minute out to imagine. After all, they survived eight weeks without Mom doing Mom. I was inspired. No more excuses. I was looking for results. I wanted to achieve the dreams inside of me. I wanted back all the pieces of me spread out all over life. Nursing, mucking and cleaning couldn't stop the dreamer that woke up inside. Who would have thought a shattered ankle could help me find me again?

I challenge you to go find your pieces. Somewhere in there is the woman you started out being, a girl who grew up dreaming, the you who had desires and passions. A you who hoped for things, who sketched out a future on your mind's note pad. It may be time for a makeover. Take a day out to do nothing but dream. You're never too old to start again, never too far gone to recalculate. Determine that a fragmented woman is an unstable women with no strength for the storms. Typically, an emotional mess.

A determined woman is confident, sure of herself, smiles and laughs. She gets puked on and keeps on going. She walks as if she is headed somewhere, because she is. She's on the road to making her dreams come true.

You're going to give the world the greatest expression of you possible, staying the woman God designed you to be, with the dreams and agenda He commissioned for your life. A you with no regrets, no "What ifs?". If you don't catch your dreams, how could you ever teach your children to follow theirs?. If you lose yourself in the mess of life, when your loved ones come looking for you, who will respond?

8.

Come Away

Mark 6;30-32. *"Then the apostles gathered to Jesus and told Him all things, both what they had done and what they had taught. **31** And He said to them, 'Come aside by yourselves to a deserted place and rest a while.' For there were many coming and going, and they did not even have time to eat. **32** So they departed to a deserted place in the boat by themselves."*

"Come aside by yourselves to a deserted place and rest a while." Jesus told His apostles this after a tremendous journey of accomplishment. They were actually excited about all they had done and all they had seen. They were ministering to the people and teaching. In other words, they were pouring themselves out. They were so busy with coming and going that eating wasn't even a priority. Why would we not take heed to this command, "Come away"? On a weekly, monthly and daily basis, we need to make time to come away. You can only imagine. Mom of twelve, an eight-horse stable, pigs and goats to boot. Pastor of a church and oh, I homeschool. I think I can responsibly say that I am busy. I read these words Jesus said, "For there were many coming and going and they did not even eat," and I see myself all over it. There were times I was so busy that eating seemed a luxury. I typically become over-worked, unfocused, and short due to the schedule my life pursues.

Jesus Himself used this method of refreshing. We read about the well-known occasion where Jesus got away in His time of agony, in the Garden of Gethsemane. He was sad and struggling with the journey ahead, and He knew that He needed to be alone to pray and intercede for Himself, work it out with the Father. He cried, He asked God if it were possible for there to be another way. But in the end he was strengthened by the fact that He was totally surrendered to the will of His Father. Before He left, He said, "Nevertheless, thy will be done."

This is a beautiful example for us in life. If we would regularly take our troubles to the Lord, cry them out and ask Him to do what only He can do, we would then be able to get up with the strength to carry on by the attitude of our hearts being yielded to His will. I think that many of the issues we face in our lives would be much easier to get through. We settle issues in our hearts when we come to Him and work them out in His presence, knowing that when all is said and done, the will of our Father will be seen in our circumstances.

I know that nothing we do in this life can be solved without His grace and mercy. This is why He instructs us, "Boldly come to his throne of grace." He desires to help us through life. In fact, He so desires to be able to walk life out with us that He planned for Jesus to return home and leave another that would walk life out with us even closer, the Holy Spirit, who would come to reside with us. God has shown me that He cares about my deepest struggles. He knows everything I think. He has shown me that He cares about the things that I used to think were small, things that I used to think He wouldn't care about. But He did. He not only cared, He showed me the way.

I remember when God started wooing me deeper into His presence. I found myself in the middle of one of the oddest seasons of my life. I knew God cared about the big things. I grew up in the church and saw many genuine miracles along the way, so I knew He could. I saw Him raise my brother up after being shot in the head with a shotgun while at work. Against the odds, my brother pulled through and he is amazing today. He crushed every medical hurdle along the way. So believing God to do the miraculous was not hard for me. He had in every way shown me His glory. If there was one thing I knew, it was that my God is a healer. He is God!!! No doubt about it!!

Conquering the issue in my heart about Him being concerned about the little things that plague us as women, as moms, as daughters, I wasn't so convinced. Some things just felt too trivial. Like God just had bigger things on His mind. But oh, how wrong I was. I saw God finding opportunities to show me that He cared about the small details. I would ask Him almost jokingly, "Lord, what do I do about this?" and He would answer. I mean I asked Him about decorating, about our bills, anything you could think of. He just showered me with answers. I would wonder about an area of my home that I was perplexed with fixing. He would show me a picture in my mind. Questions about farming — answers upon answers flooded in. God was proving His love to me in a very practical way. If I took the time to ask, He was faithful to answer. There were times He provided needs supernaturally.

But He also responded to my desires. I remember driving along one day, returning from JoAnn fabrics, picking out fabric to cover some outdoor furniture. Communing with Him in my mind, I thought, *Lord, if I could find cushions for my outdoor chairs, I could cover them too.* At the time, I had two matching chairs that had no cushions, and they could be costly. Trying to figure out a way to stretch my decoration dollars, I was seeking a way to make them for cheaper. As God is my witness, several miles further into our conversation, I found cushions, three complete sets with a sign that said, "free" on the side of the road. Amazed by His concern for my silly thoughts, I knew that there was nothing I would not bring to Him.

He tells in His word that we have not because we ask not. No answers? Have you asked Him? No grace? Have you asked? No patience? Just ask. Our Father in heaven paid an extreme price for intimacy with us. Avail yourself of Him.

I was having an absolutely rough day. I ran into the bathroom, overwhelmed with life. We had made some very bad business deals that resulted in financial strain. Desperately seeking a way out, I needed to know what we were going to do. The kids were just being wild and crazy, unaware of the fact that Mom was stressed and just needed quiet. While in the bathroom, I looked in the mirror and just started pouring out all that was going on and waiting for God to speak. I heard just this: "It's going to be okay." Simple words, but they said so much. I turned around, sat on the floor, and wrote a song:

"It's been a rough day, but it's okay, I'm looking ahead not looking behind, believing for a better day. I see the way you search for me, I see the way you smile at me, I see the way; stretched out your hands, and you're the king of the world, and I am your girl …it's gotta be okay."

I mean, when I am the daughter of God our Father, the King of the Universe, how could be we not believe that everything is going to be okay? He knows the number of the hairs on my head. No one on Earth knows the number of hairs on our head. I get it. He cares about the details. From that day on, I ran into His presence. I know that in His presence there's fullness of joy. At His right hand, pleasures forever more. You have to come away and find peace in your quiet time with Him, so He can tell you it's going to be okay.

I've learned from John Maxwell that EVERTHING RISES AND FALLS ON LEADERSHIP. As a mom, as a pastor, and on the ranch, I am a leader. It is imperative that I live by this principle. If I want to be able to have anything flow through me that is sound and stable, I have to find and make time to come aside. When I decided that spending time in God's presence was not a nice thought but a priority, I knew that I would have to get creative to consistently find a way. I sometimes take walks. I find peace and focus when I walk. I commune with the Lord and get refreshed. I'm a better mom when I return.

Focused and creative, I can tackle my day with an energy and excitement that I would not have without the walk.

There were times my only time away was grocery shopping, so I rewarded myself with a quiet lunch after I shopped. When I spent too much at the grocery store, I would go for coffee. Whatever way you find works for you will do the trick, but you must make a priority to make coming aside a part of your life. Vacations are nice. Needed, even. But regular times of coming aside, leaving the regular atmosphere, routine and people to refocus, refuel and think is the most important thing you can do for your life and those depending on you.

I remember in the early years of raising the kids, it seemed so hard to find time to come aside even to spend time with God. I would try at night when the kids were done. Every attempt failed, and the minute I would close my eyes to pray, I would fall asleep exhausted from a long day. I would sneak moments to talk to Him throughout the day. One thing that I always did was find time to talk to God while mopping, making beds and doing laundry. It seemed the perfect time to lift my children up to Him by name as I was folding their clothes and walking through their rooms. "Lord, move in their life today, Reveal Yourself to them and cover every silly thing they attempt and reveal to me anything I need to know." I found that I would have great times of refreshing surrounding cleaning and communing, and God would meet me there.

One day while cleaning and doing my normal adventures, I was walking about the house, cleaning and communing with the Lord. I heard Him say, "Go look upstairs." I went, as I had learned to trust the voice of God. When I got upstairs, I moved about the rooms, searching for what I was to be looking for. I found nothing in my immediate view, so back downstairs I headed. Before I even reached the bottom step, I heard God say go back upstairs and go in the closet. I did, and now I started to feel a little anxious, because I figured that if my heavenly Father was sending me back up there, I was going to find something. I opened the closet, went into the small crawl space behind the closet, and found a lamp that the kids had left on that was turned over on a pile of blankets, smoldering. "Thank You, Lord!!!" His faithfulness is astounding.

I say this to assure you that He knows the seasons of life you are in, and when He sees your pursuit of Him, He responds in grace. I was His daughter, and He knew I was giving all I knew to do at the time. I knew that as the kids grew older and as my responsibilities grew, I needed to "hear" God s voice, more than I needed to speak. He was faithful in answering my prayers. He said, "Make your requests known," So I did regularly. But I knew that Mark 6:30 would plague my spirit until I would find a way to come aside to quiet and hear His voice. *"So He humbled you, allowed you to hunger, and fed you with manna which you did not know nor did your fathers know, **that** He might make you know **that** man shall not **live by** bread alone; but man **lives by every word that proceeds from the mouth** of the Lord."* Deuteronomy 8:3 Bigger issues, bigger need for His presence. Things I didn't know about, but needed to know.

I wasn't going to get those answers in the quick moments, stolen moments to speak to my Dad. I needed to find a way to add significant time in my day, every day, to seek His face and hear His voice. I made up in my mind that the benefits far outweighed the so-called time loss in my mind. I had been telling myself that from the moment my feet hit the floor in the morning until they lifted into the bed at night, I was busy. Too busy and too encumbered to take time out to do "nothing." But it wasn't nothing, it was the most important thing I could have done for me and my family.

I committed to waking up and meeting with the Lord at 5:30am. I started out doing it a couple times a week. The reward was amazing. I loved the time I spent with God. He started showing me things, giving me decorating ideas, and He revealed to me hidden things in my heart. I honestly felt bad for my husband. It was the highlight of my days. I would ask Him about a problem area in my home, with little money to fix it. He would give me a picture in my mind's eye, and I realized He was giving me a vision. What I could see, I could ascribe to, and eventually reach. It was happening. Things were getting done at a rate that was exhilarating, home improvements, home school accomplishments, getting more organized.

You see, those moments with God weren't just me talking. It was God reveling to me the "whys." Why was I doing doing,

doing and not getting anywhere? Why was I not able to see the fruits of my labors in many areas of my life, though I labored? He began to show me, "You're not disciplined enough. Focus on your time management. Look at the space you're not seeing. Watch that child's routine. Look at your routine. Look at where your time is being used up. Set better boundaries." I could have never gotten all that without coming away with Him, without planning that undivided focus on Him. That 5:30 date with the King proved to be a life-changing decision. I can't begin to tell you how my routine has changed, the amount of things I am accomplishing now, in the course of the day. The wisdom I have, the insight into our future and daily issues.

My family is so much better off. They have a mom who is focused, determined, and fruitful. Remember from the earlier chapter, I mentioned that I am the conduit. If the conduit is not clear, the water begins to trickle. Floods will come forth from you when you find a way to come aside. The enemy is clever in his deception about time. We think we don't have time to come aside. We tell ourselves that there is too much to do in the day, and if I stop to "pray" it's going to take away from something else. The tithe principle covers time. So when you put God first, He multiplies everything, including your time. You end up being able to accomplish more than you would have when you were running on Dunkin, and clogged up pipes. Caffeine can't complete what the "time tithe" has instilled.

Jesus Himself came aside to replenish. What makes us think that we can pour and pour and pour and not come away to be restored? We end up doing things out of the flesh that God wants us to do out of our spirit. What do you do when you have nothing left to give? This time away has been the difference between life and death for me.

One day I woke to meet with God and it seemed just an ordinary day. One of my daily requests is that God would send angels to guard my borders, and protect my family as we carry on our daily tasks. My oldest daughter came out to ride the four-wheeler with a girlfriend. While I was in my prayer time, God had instructed me to add to my prayer, "Watch over us as we ride." Not a prayer I usually prayed. I would find out later why I needed to pray that prayer. The girls went out, but we noticed them walking back. Unsure of what had happened, my son mentioned, "I bet they crashed the four-wheeler." I looked up from doing science with the little ones to see that they looked fine, but really weren't.

I got up and went to see what happened, when I learned that indeed they did crash and the four-wheeler laid turned over in a ditch. The girls had flipped over and gone off a three-foot ravine cliff. The wheeler was turned over on my daughter when her girlfriend picked it up off her and the helmet was left lying on a concrete pipe. Not only did she lift the four-wheeler off my daughter, they walked back from about three to four acres out. They told me they were fine, just shaken up. But I didn't feel easy about it. They had plans to go out, so they were anxious to leave and continue their plans. I asked them to please just get checked out, I would feel better if they went to the hospital. Well, we came to find out that not only was she not fine, My daughters friend had broken her neck and back in five places. This could have easily been a death sentence.

God had sent His angels to do what only they could do. I believe that the enemy intended to take some lives that day, but God in His awesomeness gave us the Holy Spirit who instructs His children how to pray. Both girls are recovered and doing well. It could have been a very different scenario. God is faithful always. Even in those times we aren't. Thank God!!! But so much of what the enemy has freedom to do in our lives is simply because we give him the allowance to move freely throughout our family and life because we don't come aside. He breeds frustration in our hearts and clutters our activities. When we make coming aside a priority, God will bless and direct all our endeavors.

I have been asked by so many, "How do you do it?" Well, I'm definitely not superwoman. My life line is the Father. People are astounded at how we "afford" life. We know who our Provider is. He always makes a way out of no way when you humble yourself before Him. Seek First... your Father. And all these things, issues of life will be made straight for you. Mathew 6:33

9.

Pleasure In The Process

S arah was a woman up in years, waiting for God to do something amazing in her life. In fact, the Bible says that Sarah was "beyond" the time of her body naturally being able to produce a child. Yet God said it and she was waiting. Her conversation with the Lord was awesome. She was struggling, but wanted to believe what God had said, and this floors me. These are Sarah's words: *12 **Sarah laughed to herself**, saying, "After I have become old, shall I have pleasure, my lord being old also?"* Genesis 18:12 Wow, God not only wanted to do something amazing in her life, but He also wanted her to have pleasure. Even in her old age. Even when she thought it was just about the business. Just about the child that was destined to be the seed of nations.

The purpose was big, but God was getting at the fact that He wanted her to understand that He was concerned about her enjoying life. The journey, the process. What's your challenge you're believing for or that you're after? After all my tries, after all my disappointments, after all my failures, after everyone stopped believing in me, after it seemed like there was no way out of this life. What's your question you bring to God and say: Is it possible that God wants you to have pleasure in the process? Can you imagine that God would *not* just want you to achieve great things in life? Raise great kids, build an awesome business, but have a great time doing it. Why have we settled to go about the journey just getting by, dragging our feet and settling for drama and just good enough?

Just enough. We love just a little, for fear of losing. We forget to laugh. If I asked you when was the last time you gut laughed, what would say? I don't mean chuckled. I mean when was the last time you laughed so hard your stomach hurt? Could it be that you have not stopped to smell the roses in your life? The focus to succeed can become weighty. The drive to do more, to be more, can almost destroy our effort if we allow it to overwhelm us. Some women are gripped with nostalgia because they remember high school being so great. Or a time they went on vacation. It was the best time of their life. But it's past. What are you enjoying now? You have to keep looking forward. Keep hope alive.

I have a piece of art work that hangs in the doorway of my house that says, "This is our happily ever after." When I saw it, I knew I had to have it in my house, to remind me that the best season is always the season I'm in. The best chapter of life is always the next chapter of life. God wants His daughters to find pleasure as we give and go through the day.

My family has gone through seasons where life was so mundane. We got up, did school, Mom cleaned the house, got dinner, we had dinner at the table, washed the dishes, washed the clothes, you know the drill. But life was boring. I was bored, the kids were bored, my husband was bored. We needed to make a change. Life is a gift and an adventure, so we started one. We bought a ranch. Well, to be fair, it was an old farm house. Built in 1825, it needed a lot of work, but seemed worth the work. So we did it. We bought it. We had some Amish men come out and build a new barn. My husband, children and I built the stables inside. My mom and girlfriend even lent a hand, or hammer. It was more work than we ever imagined it was going to be. But what reward. So many times we wanted to give up and quit. The rushing to get through it was the demon we battled as we settled in and started accepting that this was going to be a process. It was not going to happen overnight, but the stalls would eventually get up and soon there would be horses in them.

Well, it happened. There are horses in those stalls. There's also a lot of work to go alongside those horses in the stalls. But I'm proud to say that today, we ride horses, four-wheelers, dirt bikes and snowmobile in the winter. Life is good. But it took work. It took making a move into something that would lend itself to enjoyment and fulfillment. Is everything perfect? No, Earth will never be. If I wanted to, I could sit and make a list of all the things that are wrong or hard or that I could worry about. But I can't imagine what life would be like had we not made this move. My family has grown closer together, through fun. My marriage is so much more enjoyable. Life just provides us with daily adventures. And we ride the wave of life. It's been said and I believe it's true: Families that play together, stay together.

God never intended life to be boring and laborious. Read this exerpt from **Ecclesiastics 8:15** — *"15 So I recommend having fun, because there is nothing better for people in this world than to eat, drink, and enjoy life. That way they will experience some happiness along with all the hard work God gives them under the sun."*

If that verse does not change your life, then I don't know what will. Life is hard. It brings challenges every day that seek to overwhelm us. We chase dreams that seem to tarry. We fight hard and sometimes lose. We get hurt and unfortunately sometimes abandoned and betrayed. We find disappointment around every corner, and have to find a way to get beyond it. Solomon knew that we can't explain life's tragedies. We don't always understand why things happen in life the way they do. Life in and of itself can be reason enough to get depressed, *if we let it*. In fact, if you don't daily seek reasons to find hope, you could be overwhelmed. But he says, there's no better way to get through the hard work God gives us to do on earth than to eat, drink and enjoy life. Not just go to church, Not just pursue things and work stuff out. He said enjoy life.

There's a role we have to play. You have to eat, drink, etc. You have to partake of fun to benefit from fun. Most of us yearn for it. We watch Facebook and see all the fun things others are doing and get resentful. When the truth is, the only thing standing between you and the same fun is *you*. I encourage my grown children to enjoy life. Travel, find good friends and read the world. Take it all in. In all your discovering of destiny and careers, deciding how much money is enough money for you to live on, make sure you don't neglect the reality of planning in living. Miley Cyrus sings, "It's all about the climb." Getting to the apex of your mountain or achievement is nothing if you haven't enjoyed the climb.

One of my very dear girlfriends had a daughter who was diagnosed with cancer at an early age. I remember talking to her on the phone every day as she would share the progress and setbacks. She would go to the hospital and have to deal with the agony of finding out that some patients? lost the fight in between visits. She was sad and the situation was difficult to walk through and difficult to hear. She remained positive the entire time. In fact, I can't remember her ever asking, "Why me? Why my daughter?" Even through her tears, they were tears of sadness and sometimes fear. But she never sold tickets to a pity party. Though I'm pretty sure watching your baby girl fight for her life would give you reason enough to do so. She preferred to hope. Every day she had a new day, she embraced it.

My husband at the same time would come home from work and he would share the terrible things that he would see at work through the course of the day. The streets were getting worse and the evil he encountered was hard to make sense of, though it was the job he signed up for and would do it all again. He believed in the need to serve and protect. I, however, was melting under the weight of how dismal life seemed. I felt terrible for both of them and wished that I could change the situations. I asked the Lord one day, "Why is life so hard?" He sent me to this scripture: *"Finally, brothers and sisters, whatever is true, whatever is noble, whatever is right, whatever is pure, whatever is lovely, whatever is admirable—if anything is excellent or praiseworthy — think about such things."*

Philippians 4:8

I needed to remind myself that with all the craziness of life, there's a choice. Ponder on the negative? Consider the positive. What we face in life, we have no control over. However, we do have control over how we face it. My friend and husband needed to talk about what they were going through. On the other hand, I had to process all that bad news, information and stories and still live life with expectation. Our human minds were not created to hold and ponder negative information with no release. We have to make up in our minds that every day, every challenge we face, we face with hope. We have to look forward to what God will do next. When life demands more of us, that's the time to fill our minds with stories of hope, miracles, healing and victories. Choosing to be encouraged.

So box up all the things that you can't carry. Wrap them up and give them to Jesus. Jesus can carry them. He said, "Give all your worries and cares to God, for He cares about you. He cares enough for you to take your worries and carry them." Tell yourself that it's time to have some fun. David talked to himself. He said, "Why, my soul, are you downcast? Why so disturbed within me? Put your hope in God, for I will yet praise him, my Savior and my God." Psalms 43:5 David wasn't having conflicts in his personality. His soul wasn't off over in another room. He had to grab ahold of his emotions and talk himself out of misery, remind himself to put his hope in God.

When life throws you a loop, when things get messy and your emotions drag you under, you have to talk yourself happy. Talk yourself into peace. Walk your emotions to the presence of the almighty God, who is able and capable of carrying the burdens we have and the challenges we face.

You may be saying to yourself, "It's just not that simple." I don't intend to make light of where you may be in your life journey today. I know there are struggles that seem to have no end, but I'd like to share one last story with you.

Hannah was a barren woman in the Bible. She too wanted a child. She, like many women in the Bible and in contemporary life, lost hope for that which she longed for. She got to the place where life just became bitter to her. She was not bitter. Life became bitter. She had no joy, everything was bland, and she was in despair. I pray that it wouldn't be an inference into scripture to assume that a woman who had no hope, and whom life had become bitter to, would not be a woman who smiled much or enjoyed the road she was on.

Have you ever felt sad or frustrated inside? Even if you said nothing about it, others around you questioned, "What was wrong?" We tell the story about what is going on inside when no words are spoken. When we think that our circle is unaware of what our soul is speaking, they see it. I have said several times, "You radiate what you feel." What's going on inside you comes through you. The taste of life had become bitter to Hannah. Life can do that to all of us. Hannah found life bitter, even though she stayed in God's presence. She frequented the temple and she cried out to God. But until she held that baby in her arms, she found no pleasure in the process. She was going to get that baby. But waiting can break down the best of us.

Proverbs 13:12 says, *"Hope deferred makes the heart sick, but a longing fulfilled is a tree of life."* If we can just learn to have fun while we wait. When the wait is over, a tree of life. I want to celebrate in the wait and celebrate in receiving.

It all starts as a decision. You and your family don't have to move or build a stable. You may just need to take that vacation you have been talking about. It might be time to have a dinner party or go dancing. If you're a crafter make it a part of your week. Whatever it is that you are going through right now, take time out to enjoy life. God is calling to remind you of your dreams and the incredible creation you are.

Woman, built with strength, creative in your thinking, power to do exploits. Nothing is impossible for you. Surely you can use a little creativity to bring fun and excitement into your journey. Pleasure into your process?

I know there are mountains to be climbed, and there's a struggle you're getting through. Children to be cared for and houses to clean. Cities to be run and companies to manage. I dare you to approach it all with a commitment to have pleasure in the process. I believe that if you are determined to enjoy life, you will. My kids can tell you, I'm liable to break out in song and dance at any given moment. When you least expect it. I'm going to do something weird and obnoxiously fun to stir up what's stagnant. I'll throw on some music and whistle while I work. If you started eating, drinking and having fun while you do all that God has commissioned you to do with your life, you will shine brighter, go farther and laugh louder.

You want to be beautiful? Live happy. You want to be effective? Be happy. There's no greater accessory you can apply than happiness. What do you have to lose? The work isn't going anywhere and you are going to do it anyway. You might as well ENJOY IT!

When we moved into this house, there was a barn that the previous owner donated to the Quakers. It was falling apart, but it had a lot of history attached to it, as well as sentimental value. The day they came to move the barn across the street, I went as a field trip for the kids to watch the move. I found out that Susan B. Anthony spoke in that barn and held rallies there. This young, amazing woman challenged and inspired change. She championed women's rights to vote and own property, and fought to abolish slavery. I'm inspired when I think about the fact that here I sit, inspiring women as well, from the same location. I'm honored to be walking and living on the same property where she advocated for women's rights.

I am writing to encourage and inspire you from rich soil, with a message of hope. Carry the fire. Go inspire. Go be everything you know is given to you to do and desire to be. If the great women of the past could reach down inside themselves, find significance inside to make their mark, if all the women of faith could rise from the difficulties that opposed them and touched generations, then so can you. You are a woman.